Wha' Hoppen?

A Politically Incorrect Look Back at the 2016 Presidential Campaigns, the Election and Aftermath

---

Katrina Vasilnova

Wha' Hoppen?

ISBN 13: 978-0692978870
ISBN 10: 0692978879

Sky Scientific Press
PO Box 7067
Brookings, Oregon 97415
www.skyscientific.com

CONTENTS

AUTHOR'S NOTE

In researching, writing and reviewing the material presented in this book, I was often faced with the task of deciding which of two or more conflicting claims or narratives best represented the truth surrounding an issue. While every effort was made to consistently present what was believed to be the truth—or most nearly the truth—I sought to include credible opposing opinions or mitigating details where appropriate.

Katrina Vasilnova
k_vasilnova@protonmail.com

1.
In the Beginning . . .

IT WOULD BE REASONABLE FOR YOU to assume that this first chapter of *Wha' Hoppen?* is all about the early days of the political campaigns leading up to the 2016 presidential election, as the chapter title implies. We'll get to all that—in due course—but first you need to know how and why this book project came about.

Larry, my literary agent was less than encouraging when I first proposed this project in early December 2016—less than one month after the votes were counted.

"The election is over," he argued, "and even if more than half the voters in the country feel we were cheated, no one cares anymore why or how it happened."

Larry was always a glass-half-empty kind of guy, which struck me as uncharacteristic of anyone with a successful career devoted to promoting the work of others, but Larry was very successful, nevertheless. You would be impressed if you saw the list of political topic writers that he represented. I was lucky to have him, I thought.

During our meeting that day, I didn't try to convince Larry that—contrary to his usual spot-on logic—this time he was all wrong. In my unstated opinion, it was *exactly* the right time for such a book. On my way home that day I kept replaying his words over and over in my head—the part about "more than half the voters in the country" feeling cheated, with Larry counting himself among them.

It seemed odd to me that Larry was pre-occupied with the notion that if not for those few pesky clauses in the Constitution about the Electoral College, that Hillary Clinton would be the rightful winner and president-elect.

WE LEARNED ON FEBRUARY 1, 2017, that Simon & Schuster would be publishing a new book by Hillary Clinton, scheduled for a fall release date. Characterized as a memoir, sources close to Mrs Clinton reported that it would include the former candidate's personal thoughts concerning the 2016 campaign and election.

Nearly six months would pass before the title of Hillary's new book was disclosed. It was unclear why it took so long to come up with the title, *What Happened*, but it took far less time for "alternate" titles to appear on Twitter and internet blogs. Within a few hours the hashtag *#BetterNamesForHillarysBook* began trending with alternate titles such as *Crime and No Punishment* and *How to Lose Elections and Alienate People*.

I saw Larry at a social event in early August 2017—months after the election—and casually reminded him of my earlier project proposal and his distinctly negative response to the idea back in December. Before responding, he looked about for anyone within earshot nearby, then took my hand and led me to a vacant corner of the room.

"I'm sorry, Kat," he said, "but I really didn't believe that the timing was right back then for a conservative postmortem of the election—too many frayed nerves."

"And what about now?" I asked. He looked away momentarily, then frowned and raised his voice.

"You wouldn't want ride on the coattails of Hillary's new book, would you? Like all those parasites who came out with titles similar to *Fifty Shades of Grey* after that book made it big?" His demeanor had changed almost instantly. He was angry, and for the first time I began to understand what was going on inside Larry and so many others in the country.

My relationship with Larry had always been strictly business. We rarely discussed politics, but anyone with ears to hear would have known that he held very liberal political views. But politics had always been far down on the list of items that drove him; that is, until the results of the 2016 presidential election were known.

I saw it in many close acquaintances who had supported Hillary. I saw it in most members of the media and Hollywood. Something had been triggered in the psyche of so many on the Liberal Left and among Establishment Republicans. Maybe it was the shock of an election loss that everyone believed Hillary would win. Maybe it was not because Hillary lost, but because she lost to Donald Trump.

In trying to explain the extreme emotional criticism surrounding the George W. Bush Administration in 2003, author and political commentator Charles Krauthammer coined the expression "Bush

Derangement Syndrome." He wrote in a column:

> BUSH DERANGEMENT SYNDROME: THE ACUTE ONSET OF PARANOIA IN OTHERWISE NORMAL PEOPLE IN REACTION TO THE POLICIES, THE PRESIDENCY—NAY—THE VERY EXISTENCE OF GEORGE W. BUSH.

Consequently, I was not surprised when the term, "Trump Derangement Syndrome," came into use to describe the state of mind of those engaged in the highly emotional criticism of Donald Trump and his administration. When I left the social event that day, I knew only one thing for certain: I was going to need a new agent.

2.
O Bernie, Where Art Thou?

IN HER RECENT MEMOIR, HILLARY Clinton cited multiple events and issues she believed responsible for her election loss with several attributed to Bernie Sanders. She said that during the primary season Sanders disparaged her character by suggesting that she was corrupt—having been "bought and paid for" by Wall Street. Hillary claimed that Bernie's attacks paved the way for Donald Trump's "Crooked Hillary" campaign.

After winning the California primary election on June 7, 2016, Hillary Clinton declared herself the Democratic Party nominee for the presidential election, with a presumed delegate vote count about 400 greater than the 2,383 needed to win. Bernie vowed to fight on to the Democratic National Convention that was still more than six weeks away, but at a joint rally held in Portsmouth, New Hampshire, on July 12, 2016, Sanders disappointed many of his followers by proceeding to endorse and declare his support for Clinton. On the first day of the Democratic National Convention in Philadelphia on July 25, he called on his supporters to vote for Hillary.

And yet during a stop at ABC's "The View" on September 13, 2017, as a part of her book tour, Hillary insisted that Senator Sanders did not give her the "respect" she deserved during the campaign. Clinton said:

> I KNOW WHAT IT'S LIKE TO LOSE. I LOST IN 2008 TO PRESIDENT OBAMA. AS SOON AS I LOST I ENDORSED HIM. I WORKED HARD FOR HIM. I WAS ARGUING WITH MY SUPPORTERS AT THE DENVER CONVENTION IN 2008 WHY THEY HAD TO STOP COMPLAINING ABOUT HOW I DIDN'T WIN AND TO GET OUT AND WORK FOR PRESIDENT OBAMA, AND I DIDN'T GET THAT RESPECT.

The truth is that Bernie Sanders wholeheartedly supported Hillary Clinton well before and after the 2016 Democratic National Convention. In the six weeks immediately preceding the general election, Bernie gave speeches at more than thirty "Get Out the Vote" rallies in support of Hillary Clinton.

It is true that Sanders disagreed with many of Clinton's policies and believed she was too close to her Wall Street donors, but he nonetheless worked diligently on her behalf in hopes of keeping Donald Trump from the presidency. Sanders spent much of his time persuading supporters—many of whom were very much opposed to Hillary—to reconsider and vote for her.

Bernie's supporters were angry; first angry at Bernie for quitting early when he had promised he would take the fight to the convention floor, but angrier at the DNC for its treatment of Sanders.

On July 22, 2016, just three days before the Democratic National Convention, WikiLeaks published nearly 20,000 hacked email messages sent to and from staff members of the Democratic National Committee. The content in several of the leaked messages made it clear that key members of the DNC staff had actively engaged in sabotage against Bernie Sanders' campaign. It was a huge embarrassment to the DNC and resulted in the following formal apology issued to Senator Sanders and his supporters on July 25:

> ON BEHALF OF EVERYONE AT THE DNC, WE WANT TO OFFER A DEEP AND SINCERE APOLOGY TO SENATOR SANDERS, HIS SUPPORTERS, AND THE ENTIRE DEMOCRATIC PARTY FOR THE INEXCUSABLE REMARKS MADE OVER EMAIL. THESE COMMENTS DO NOT REFLECT THE VALUES OF THE DNC OR OUR STEADFAST COMMITMENT TO NEUTRALITY DURING THE NOMINATING PROCESS. . . . THE DNC IS TAKING APPROPRIATE ACTION TO ENSURE IT NEVER HAPPENS AGAIN.

DNC Chairperson Debbie Wasserman Schultz had resigned the day before the apology letter was released.

A second reason why Sanders' supporters were angry was due to the convention delegate count and influence of the "superdelegates." The latter are voting delegates to the convention from among Democratic Party officials and activists.

Convention superdelegates were free to support any candidate of their choosing with their vote and comprise about fifteen percent of the total voting delegates at the convention. The remaining 85 percent are "pledged" delegates who are obliged to cast their vote—at least for the first ballot of the convention—for the winner of the primary election or caucus in their respective state.

On the eve of the convention, the Associated Press estimated that 609 superdelegates had expressed support for and were expected to vote for Hillary Clinton, with only 47 for Bernie Sanders. With Clinton and Sanders having 2,205 and 1,846 pledged delegates, respectively, it was clear that it was Clinton's clear advantage in superdelegates that would put her over the top—the 2,383 delegate votes needed to win the nomination.

Now, Hillary supporters are quick to remind us that she was the only real Democrat campaigning to become the Democratic nominee for president. Sanders had consistently represented the state of Vermont in the House of Representatives and the Senate as an Independent, so it would be expected that Hillary would be the favored candidate among the Democratic Party officials and activists that make up the superdelegates. The problem is that the large number of superdelegates gave Mrs Clinton a huge lead even before the first ballot was cast, furthering the notion in the minds of Sanders' supporters that the convention was rigged in Hillary's favor.

When most party officials and activists who are superdelegates support a single candidate, it is hard for any opposing candidate—however popular—to overcome the delegate gap. There was such an outcry during the 2016 Convention that party officials subsequently voted to limit the number of unpledged delegates for future conventions to only a third of the superdelegates. The Republican Party already limits the number of unpledged delegates—equivalent to superdelegates—to not more than three per state.

And what of Mrs Clinton's claim that after her loss to Barack Obama in the 2008 Democratic campaign that she worked diligently to help Obama win the presidential election? It is true—she did help Barack Obama beat John McCain, the Republican nominee, with endorsements and personal appearances on his behalf. Coincidentally, the president-elect helped Clinton pay off her campaign debt—estimated at ten to twenty million dollars—by calling upon his own donors to contribute to her campaign coffers. For the next four years, Hillary Clinton served as secretary of state in the Obama Administration.

HILLARY APOLOGISTS WOULD ARGUE that there is incontrovertible evidence that Sanders' support for her was insufficient or ineffectual, particularly in persuading his supporters to vote for Mrs Clinton in the general election. The 2016 Cooperative Congressional Election Survey of fifty thousand voters conducted after the presidential election showed that up to twelve percent of former Sanders supporters cast their vote for Donald Trump. Looking at individual states, the data show that if the Sanders-to-Trump voters in Wisconsin, Michigan and Pennsylvania had instead voted for Clinton (or even stayed home and not voted) then Hillary Clinton would have prevailed and won the electoral votes for all three states and the presidency.

It is not known how many of the Sanders-to-Trump supporters were Republicans, Independents or possibly Libertarian voters who came to appreciate and eventually support Bernie Sanders' candidacy. It seems unreasonable to have expected Sanders to succeed in convincing all of these voters to switch their support to a candidate like Hillary Clinton when it is unlikely that they would have voted for Hillary if Bernie had never entered the race.

In a Fivethirtyeight.com feature story by Harry Enten dated August 8, 2016, it was estimated that up to one-third of Bernie's supporters were not backing Mrs Clinton. The article was based upon data from several polls taken immediately after the Democratic Convention. Over the next three months, Bernie's efforts helped bring most of those voters into Hillary's camp. Instead of being critical of his support for her campaign she should have expressed some gratitude for his efforts.

3.
Show Me the Money!

I BELIEVE THAT MOST VOTERS HAVE no problem with politicians who have become wealthy selling books or running a business, or even for accepting reasonable honoraria for speaking engagements. What they object to are politicians who receive huge sums of cash under circumstances that do not pass the "smell test." A typical example is when there is an appearance of influence peddling—when the politician or a family member is paid by someone or some group looking for a ruling, contract or other favor that the politician might be able to deliver.

Donald Trump and his family members have benefited financially under circumstances that some might characterize as questionable. Included are the following:

- The Donald J. Trump Foundation was established in 1988 with headquarters in New York City. Critics have charged that Mr Trump has used as much as $250,000 in foundation money to settle legal disputes. He was also criticized for a $25,000 donation given to a group supporting Florida Attorney General Pam Bondi in her reelection campaign. The donation arrived just a few days before a Florida investigation into Trump University was suspended by the state attorney general's office. Trump and Bondi were subsequently cleared of any wrong doing when the state attorney looking into the matter wrote that "The majority of the complaint consists of insinuation without any material evidence in support." The Trump University matter was finally resolved in November 2016, when Trump agreed to pay $25 million in settlements to the plaintiffs in multiple lawsuits related to the school.

- The Trump election campaign spent more than $55,000 buying copies of his own book, *Crippled America: How to Make America Great Again.* The books were given to delegates at the Republican National Convention.

Presumably, Donald Trump earned royalty payments for these book sales.

- In January 2017, the White House website biography of first lady Melania Trump made reference to her jewelry line and that it was for sale on the commercial QVC shopping channel. Critics complained that it represented continuing attempts by Donald Trump to financially benefit from his elected position. In response to the criticism, the mention of jewelry available on QVC was removed from the website.

- According to a January 25, 2017, CNBC report, the one-time initiation fee for membership in the club at the Trump Mar-a-Lago resort in Palm Beach was reportedly raised from $100,000 to $200,000. The increase was effective on January 1, 2017.

- In February 2017, the Federal Election Commission reported that payments in excess of $12.8 million were made by the Trump Election Campaign to companies owned by Donald Trump or family members. The payments were for campaign expenses for travel, including food and lodging, as well as rent, utilities, and office supplies. It is assumed that the payments were for legitimate expenses of the campaign, and if so, the fact that the campaign chose to use vendors with which it was most familiar should not have raised any concerns.

- According to a May 7, 2017, CNN Money report, Jared Kushner's sister Nicole Meyer was offering investors in Beijing an opportunity to invest in a new Kushner-family real estate development in New Jersey. As an inducement, investors able to plunk down $500,000 or more would be eligible for a coveted EB-5 investor visa that would enable them to qualify for legal residence as an immigrant to the U.S. The implication was clear that the Kushner influence in the White House would facilitate the granting of the visa. When the details of the promotion were reported by CNN, the offers were suspended.

Candidates for the 2016 presidential election were required to submit personal financial disclosures before a May 15, 2016, deadline. The Clintons declared their calendar year 2015 income of about $12 million and Donald Trump reported $557 million for the same period. Bernie Sanders requested and received two 45-day extensions to submit, and then advised the Federal Election Commission that he would not be providing a financial disclosure as he was—by that time—no longer a candidate.

It should be obvious to any clear thinking individual that someone with an annual income of a half-billion dollars and net worth purportedly as much as $4 billion is unlikely to make controversial decisions for the express purpose of adding thousands or even a few million dollars to his income.

As further evidence that financial gain was not a motivating factor in his decision to run for office, President Trump donated the first quarter of his annual $400,000 salary to the department of interior, earmarked for the National Park Service. The department of education received the full donation of his salary for the second quarter of his presidency, and the president has continued to donate his entire executive salary throughout his first term in office.

THE CLINTONS HAVE BENEFITED FROM several questionable financial dealings over the past four decades, but have typically downplayed their significance. In a June

2014 interview with Diane Sawyer, Hillary Clinton was asked about her financial situation and reports that she had earned millions in speaking fees. Hillary responded, "You have no reason to remember, but we came out of the White House not only dead broke, but in debt." She added, "We had no money when we got there, and we struggled to piece together the resources for mortgages for houses, for Chelsea's education. It was not easy. Bill has worked really hard. And it's been amazing to me. He's worked very hard."

The facts are that the Clintons purchased two homes before leaving the White House: In 1999, they bought a five-bedroom home in Chappaqua, New York, for $1.7 million, and in December 2000, a seven-bedroom house in Washington, D.C., for $2.85 million with an $855,000 cash down payment. Thus, upon leaving the White House, the Clintons were indeed "in debt," in consideration of the property mortgages, but few would disagree that the term "dead broke" is an inaccurate and misleading characterization of the Clintons' financial condition as of January 2001. On several subsequent occasions the Clintons defended the "dead broke" description of their finances but acknowledged that the statement may have been "in-artful."

By 2004, the Clintons had erased their debts. Hillary Clinton was ranked as the 10th-wealthiest member of the Senate, with a net worth in excess of $10 million, thanks in part to an $8 million advance for her autobiography, *Living History*, published by Simon & Schuster. After leaving office in 2001, Bill Clinton earned $17 million in speaking fees for the 97 speeches he gave up until December 2003. Nearly all of Bill Clinton's speeches were given outside the U.S. In addition, he received a $10 million advance for his autobiography, *My Life*, published by the Knopf Publishing Group. It was a true statement by Hillary when she said, "Bill has worked really hard."

The following are details of some of the financial dealings that have been a source of concern among many of those critical of the Clintons throughout the years:

- Hillary Clinton opened a commodities trading account in 1978 with $1,000 just before Bill Clinton became governor of Arkansas. Over the next nine months, the account grew in value to more than $100,000 thanks to guidance and assistance provided by James Blair, a family friend and attorney. There was evidence that several trading rules were violated, but no government investigation regarding the matter has ever been conducted. It has been estimated that the odds of a trader making those gains in a fair market during the period in question were about one in more than thirty-one trillion. In an April 10, 1994, *Newsweek* article by Mark Hosenball, the author explained:

THE BROKER, BUYING FUTURES, HITS THE JACKPOT ON SOME CONTRACTS AND LOSES ON OTHERS WITHIN THE SAME DAY. AT THE CLOSE, HE 'ALLOCATES' WINNING CONTRACTS TO SOME CLIENTS AND LOSING CONTRACTS TO OTHERS. ONLY THE BROKER KNOWS HOW THE ALLOCATION WAS MADE, SO HE IS ABLE TO REWARD SOME CLIENTS AT THE EXPENSE OF OTHERS.

According to the White House, Mrs Clinton had no knowledge of contract allocations associated with her trading account.

- In 1978 Bill and Hillary Clinton borrowed $203,000 together with Jim and Susan McDougal to purchase 230 acres of undeveloped land in Arkansas along the White River. The couples together formed the Whitewater Development Corporation with a plan to subdivide the land into individual lots for vacation homes. The Whitewater project failed due to steadily rising interest rates which effectively prevented potential buyers from purchasing lots and financing any construction.

What followed was a head-splitting and impossibly convoluted series of related events involving the McDougal's Madison Guarantee Savings and Loan and a real estate venture known as Castle Grande. McDougal's bank failed and was taken over by the Resolution Trust Corporation. Hillary Clinton, employed by the Rose Law Firm in Littlerock, represented the Castle Grande project which itself failed in 1989 with an estimated cost to the government of approximately $4 million. The subsequent failure of Madison Guarantee Savings and Loan cost the government $70 million in loan guarantees.

After investigations and indictments, some fifteen individuals were convicted, including Jim Guy Tucker, who had become governor of Arkansas after Bill Clinton. Susan McDougal refused to answer questions under oath about the Clinton's involvement in Whitewater and was sentenced to 18 months in prison for contempt of court, but was eventually pardoned by President Clinton before he left office. It is believed that the Clintons lost about $50,000 on their Whitewater investment, but they were never charged with a crime.

• Hillary Clinton began her official public service political career as Senator for the state of New York in 2001, just before Bill and Hillary left the White House on January 20th of that year. She left the Senate at about the midpoint of her second term to accept the position of secretary of state in the Obama Administration after losing her bid to become the Democratic Party nominee for president in 2008. Hillary was secretary of state until February 2013. Two months later she gave her first paid corporate speech to the financial giant, Morgan Stanley, in Washington, D.C., for which she received $225,000. Over the next two years Mrs Clinton gave 90 more corporate speeches in the U.S., Canada and Mexico for which she earned an additional \$21.5 million.

There had been numerous requests by Bernie Sanders and others for Hillary to release transcripts of her Wall Street speeches, but no transcripts were released. In October 2016 WikiLeaks published partial transcripts contained in John Podesta's hacked emails. Not surprisingly, a predominant theme of her speeches was that, in her opinion, bankers were best positioned to reform the U.S. financial sector. In her memoir, *What Happened*, Hillary admits that the dozens of speeches she gave to Wall Street corporations was a mistake. She wrote:

JUST BECAUSE MANY FORMER GOVERNMENT OFFICIALS HAVE BEEN PAID LARGE FEES TO GIVE SPEECHES, I SHOULDN'T HAVE ASSUMED IT WOULD BE OKAY FOR ME TO DO IT. ESPECIALLY AFTER THE FINANCIAL CRISIS OF 2008-2009, I SHOULD HAVE REALIZED IT WOULD BE BAD 'OPTICS' AND STAYED AWAY FROM ANYTHING HAVING TO DO WITH WALL STREET. I DIDN'T. THAT'S ON ME.

- The Clintons are associated with two similarly-named philanthropic entities, the "Clinton Foundation" and the "Clinton Family Foundation." The latter is much smaller and has not suffered nearly as much negative publicity as the far larger Clinton Foundation. In recent years, the Clintons have donated about ten percent of their annual income to the Clinton Family Foundation, and they reportedly take no income from either foundation. The Clinton Family Foundation has made significant dollar donations to the Clinton Foundation in recent years.

4.
Charity Begins at Home

CRITICS OF MRS CLINTON'S CAMPAIGN for the presidency have stated that the public perception of the Clinton Foundation and Hillary's association with it had significant negative impact on her appeal as a candidate during the weeks and months leading up to the presidential election.

The Clinton Foundation was established in 1997 by Bill Clinton. According to the foundation's website, the former president's vision was for "a nongovernmental organization that could leverage the unique capacities of governments, partner organizations, and other individuals to address rising inequalities and deliver tangible results that improve people's lives." Through 2016, it is estimated that the foundation raised $2 billion, with annual revenues in excess of $200 million.

Unlike philanthropic organizations that accept donations and issue grants of funds to other charities, the Clinton Foundation carries out many of its own programs, made possible by a staff of 2,000 employees in the U.S. and several foreign countries. Among the list of Foundation programs are the Clinton Global Initiative, Clinton Health Access Initiative, Disaster Relief and the Clinton Climate Initiative.

The Foundation has been unfairly criticized by Carly Fiorina and others who claim that only a small percentage of revenue actually goes toward charitable works. As evidence, the CARLY for America Super PAC cited the Foundation's 2013 IRS Informational Tax Form 990 which reported that the Clinton Foundation disbursed only $9 million in grants while receiving $149 million in donations. It was claimed that with only six percent of revenue going toward grants, that "there really isn't anything that can be categorized as charitable." But because it is an "operating" foundation, most charitable work is conducted through Clinton Foundation programs performed by foundation employees.

CharityWatch is an independent charity watchdog organization whose top rated charities spend 75% or more of their budgets on programs. A thorough analysis by CharityWatch that included the "in-house" charitable work as well as grants showed that the Clinton Foundation effectively directed about 89 percent of revenues to what is broadly characterized as "charitable work." Included, however, are some expenses that might be considered as unnecessarily extravagant, such as chartered aircraft and first class air tickets and accommodations provided for Clinton family members and Foundation officials and friends.

There have been other examples of programs or specific events that have raised ethical issues with respect to the Clinton Foundation:

- The Clinton Global Initiative, an important component program of the Clinton Foundation, has directed millions of dollars in support to help enable women's economic and political empowerment through a program known as the Global Fund for Women. While applauding the goals of this program, the foundation has been criticized for accepting tens of millions of dollars in donations from the governments of Qatar, Kuwait and Saudi Arabia—countries with a continuing history of treating women as second-class citizens.

- In January 12, 2010, a magnitude 7.0 earthquake struck the island nations of Haiti and Dominican Republic. The quake was centered just fifteen miles west of Port-au-Prince, Haiti's capital, and caused widespread death and devastation. As many as 300,000 perished and 1.5 million people were left destitute. Countries and philanthropic organizations from around the world donated over $10 billion in aid, and Bill Clinton became the designated United Nations representative for directing the disbursement of international funds.

    The state department, headed by Hillary Clinton at that time, was responsible for U.S. aid management for Haiti disaster relief. It has been reported that contractors who had connections with the former president were identified in the state department's approved contractor lists as FOBs (Friends of Bill) and were afforded special consideration in the awarding of contracts. In the months and years that followed, noncompetitive contracts were issued to several companies and individuals who made sizable donations to the Clinton Foundation.

In his book, *Hillary's America: The Secret History of the Democratic Party,* author Dinesh D'Souza provides several examples of fraud, corruption and cronyism surrounding the Clintons' role in Haitian disaster relief, including the following:

o   A UN relief contract was issued to the construction firm, Clayton Homes, a Berkshire Hathaway company owned by Warren Buffet. Buffett supported the Clinton Global Initiative and has made generous donations to the Clinton Foundation. After the contract was awarded to Clayton Homes, bypassing any competitive bidding process, the company built and delivered temporary housing structures that some have charged were found to be structurally unsound and unsafe due to poor construction and outgassing of the insulation materials that were used.

o Digicel is a telecom company owned by a close friend of the Clintons and a Clinton Foundation contributor. Digicel distributed thousands of phones to Haitian citizens, paid for with U.S. taxpayer dollars and administered through Hillary Clinton's state department. Digicel was able to provide billed cellular phone service to most of the population of Haiti and has become one of the largest telecom firms in the Caribbean.

o Because of the Clintons' influence with the Haitian Government, an American mining company, VCS, was able to secure a lucrative gold mining permit in Haiti after Hugh Rodham was added to the company's advisory board. As a former private detective and prison guard, Rodham had no mining experience, but he is the brother of Hillary Clinton.

Now, more than seven years after the earthquake and despite more than $13 billion in provided funding, much of the Haitian population continues to suffer.

- An early claim that the Clinton Foundation contributed $2 million to a private company, Energy Pioneer Solutions, was denied by the company founder and former Democratic congressional candidate, Scott Kleeb. It appears instead that Bill Clinton and the Clinton Global Initiative only *connected* Kleeb with wealthy friends of the Clinton Foundation who were willing to invest in EPS. It is true, however, that in 2010, Bill Clinton promoted the approval of a U.S. department of energy federal stimulus grant in the amount of $812,000 for the company.

- While Hillary supporters in the media sometimes limit coverage or choose to completely ignore charges of influence peddling or other corruption associated with the Clintons, the Uranium One issue elicited an enormous defensive response from the left. An internet search of the subject returns a cascade of sympathetic articles, including multiple and often redundant search results from independent fact-checking sites.

    Recall the charge that Hillary's state department approved the sale of Uranium One, a Canadian company that controlled 20 percent of U.S. uranium production, to Rosatom, a company run by the Russian State Nuclear Agency. In reviewing criticism directed at this charge it was learned that the state department was only one of eight or nine government agencies that had to approve the deal. However, as pointed out in a March 2017 article at Breitbart.com, Mrs Clinton "was the only agency head whose family foundation received $145 million in donations from multiple people connected to the uranium deal. . . ."

The New York Times reported that even the family foundation of Uranium One's chairman made $2.35 million in donations to the Clinton Foundation. In an agreement with the Obama Administration, it was understood that Secretary of State Hillary Clinton was to keep all Clinton Foundation business at "arm's-length" and to take steps to assure that all donations to the Clinton Foundation were properly reported. It has been reported that some questionable donations were funneled through a Canadian office of the Clinton Foundation in order to skirt disclosure requirements.

An April 2015 article from *The New York Times* reported that "shortly after the Russians announced their intention to acquire a majority stake in Uranium One, Mr Clinton received $500,000 for a Moscow speech from a Russian investment bank with links to the Kremlin that was promoting Uranium One stock." The payment was two times the ex-president's usual fee earned for a speech.

Supporters of the Clintons and the Clinton Foundation argued that according to the U.S. Nuclear Regulatory Commission, there was no risk that uranium mined under the deal would leave the country because Uranium One was never granted an export license. However, the owner of the Wyoming parcel of land for which Uranium One owned the mining rights stated that yellowcake from his property was routinely packed into drums and trucked off to a processing plant in Canada. After processing, it could be sent back to the U.S. or to any number of foreign destinations. Yellowcake is an oxide of uranium produced from uranium ore at the mine site.

LITTLE NEW INFORMATION CONCERNING the Uranium One matter was forthcoming until October 2017 when it was learned that federal authorities had an eye-witness account and documents attributed to an undercover agent confirming the Uranium One bribery and corruption allegations. In an October 17, 2017, article at The Hill by John Solomon and Alison Spann, the authors wrote:

> FEDERAL AGENTS USED A CONFIDENTIAL U.S. WITNESS WORKING INSIDE THE RUSSIAN NUCLEAR INDUSTRY TO GATHER EXTENSIVE FINANCIAL RECORDS, MAKE SECRET RECORDINGS AND INTERCEPT EMAILS AS EARLY AS 2009 THAT SHOWED MOSCOW HAD COMPROMISED AN AMERICAN URANIUM TRUCKING FIRM WITH BRIBES AND KICKBACKS IN VIOLATION OF THE FOREIGN CORRUPT PRACTICES ACT, FBI AND COURT DOCUMENTS SHOW. BUT THE OBAMA ADMINISTRATION ALLOWED THE DEAL TO MOVE FORWARD ANYWAY.

It was subsequently learned that the Obama Justice Department under Attorney General Loretta Lynch had insisted that the undercover witness sign a non-disclosure agreement (NDA) that would preclude disclosure of information about the case to any third party. The NDA effectively prevented the witness from testifying before Congress until the witness was released from the NDA by Attorney General Jeff Sessions' Justice Department on October 25, 2017.

According to an NBC report released on October 23, 2017, special counsel Robert Mueller was looking into activities of the Podesta Group and one-time Trump campaign chair Paul Manafort related to the their independent activities associated with former Ukrainian government officials. The Podesta Group is a lobbying firm headed by Tony Podesta, brother of Hillary Clinton's campaign chairman John Podesta.

It has been reported that the Podesta Group received $90,000 from Uranium One. It was known that the Podesta Group was the subject of a legal inquiry for failure to register as an international agent in a timely fashion. It is interesting to note that one of the charges resulting in Paul Manafort's arrest, conviction and subsequent incarceration was his failure to complete the required registration until June 2017.

5.
Whose Fault Is It, Anyway?

I HAD LUNCH WITH A FRIEND TWO weeks after Hillary's memoir was released, and she asked me, "Why do you think that she blamed everyone but herself for losing the election?"

I replied, "I don't think that's entirely true."

"What do you mean?" she asked. "I've read lots of reviews of that book, and just about every one of them criticizes Hillary for claiming she would have won if so-and-so hadn't done this-or-that."

I had to laugh about the way my friend phrased it, but then I said, "It's true, she did blame a lot of other people and events for losing, but she didn't hold herself entirely blameless." I then went on to mention some of Hillary's self-acknowledged mistakes and missteps that she wrote about. When I got home, I looked for more and found several:

- By way of accepting overall responsibility for the election loss, she wrote, "I go back over my own shortcomings and the mistakes we made. I take responsibility for all of them. You can blame the data, blame the message, blame anything you want — but I was the candidate. It was my campaign. Those were my decisions."

- She "almost" accepted responsibility when she wrote, "I do think it's fair to say there was a fundamental mismatch between how I approach politics and what a lot of the country wanted to hear in 2016."

- Mrs Clinton's Wall Street speeches were mentioned previously in Chapter 3. Recall that Hillary wrote in her memoir, "Just because many former government officials have been paid large fees to give speeches, I shouldn't have assumed it would be okay for me to do it. Especially after the financial crisis of 2008-2009, I should have realized it would be bad 'optics' and stayed away from anything having to do with Wall Street. I didn't. That's on me."

- Clinton calls her decision to use a private email server while secretary of state a "boneheaded mistake." She also said, "Right off the bat, let me say again that yes, the decision to use personal email instead of an official government account was mine and mine alone. I own that. I never meant to mislead anyone, never kept my email use secret, and always took classified information seriously."

- A month before the election, during an NBC-hosted event aboard the *USS Intrepid*, Matt Lauer was interviewing candidates about their foreign policy positions. During the Clinton interview he questioned the candidate about the email scandal. In her book Hillary wrote, "Here's another example where I remained polite, albeit exasperated, and played the political game as it used to be, not as it had become. That was a mistake."

- Regarding the damage from her often-quoted statement about "deplorables" she wrote, "I regret handing Trump a political gift with my 'deplorables' comment. I know that a lot of well-intentioned people were insulted because they misunderstood me to be criticizing all Trump voters. I'm sorry about that." But then it seems she is compelled to add, "But too many of Trump's core supporters do hold views that I find—there's no other word for it—deplorable."

After looking over my compiled list of instances where Hillary accepts at least partial responsibility for her loss, I have to concede that her mea culpas seem to carry a sort of self-exonerating quality about them, leaving the reader with much the same uneasy feeling as the recipient of a "left-handed" complement. I'll be sure to tell my friend when I see her again.

6.
Shut Up and Sing*

I WAS SORRY TO SEE SO MANY WOMEN demonstrating at the 2017 Women's March in Washington D.C. against the new Administration, just one day after the inauguration of Donald Trump. The Washington march drew over 400,000 participants with an estimated five million attending at over 600 scheduled events worldwide. The Washington D.C. protest was the largest since the anti-Vietnam War demonstrations from more than 40 years ago. Although the stated intent of the rallies was to promote women's rights and a list of other popular liberal causes, it was clearly aimed at the policies and positions—stated or imagined—of the new president.

It was painful for me to hear a few celebrity women, whose talents I have admired over the years, making such hateful and disparaging remarks about my president. We watched as the media repeatedly played the video clip of Madonna as she lamented, "Yes, I'm angry, yes, I'm outraged, yes I have thought an awful lot about blowing up the White House, but I know that this won't change anything." And who could forget actress Ashley Judd reciting Nina Donovan's "I am a Nasty Woman" poem at the same event?

Since then we've heard Johnny Depp ask the audience at the Glastonbury film event in the UK, "When was the last time an actor assassinated a president?" Depp then added, "I want to clarify. I'm not an actor. I lie for a living. However, it's been a while, and maybe it's time." Depp apologized for the comment the very next day, saying, "I apologize for the bad joke I attempted last night in poor taste about President Trump. It did not come out as intended, and I intended no malice. I was only trying to amuse, not to harm anyone."

Liberal singers and actors criticizing and poking fun at causes or political figures with whom they disagree is nothing new. In September 2000, the actress Julia Roberts spoke at a New York fund raiser on behalf of the Gore-Lieberman presidential ticket. "'Republican' comes in the dictionary just after 'reptile' and just above 'repugnant,'" Roberts announced and then added, "I looked up 'Democrat.' It's 'of the people, by the people, for the people.'" Of course, the audience cheered wildly as she spoke.

As avid consumers of music, film and television, most politically conservative members of the public—including myself— were willing to ignore the somewhat irritating comments made by those liberal stars. Even as the comments became more frequent and strident we still continued to listen and watch. But since the November 2016 election, the commentary has devolved into the hateful remarks that we hear reported on the news nearly every day.

I can only conclude that Trump Derangement Syndrome has become epidemic. The disorder also seems to have undergone a sort of mutation in that in addition to the previous symptoms, those afflicted most recently have totally lost any semblance of a sense of humor.

I have begun to see a change in attitude among conservative consumers of the arts: more than ever, many of us are no longer listening or watching. It seems curious to me that singers, actors, other celebrities and even some company CEOs are willing to alienate up to half of their paying customers with some injudicious piece of rhetoric. For example, GrubHub CEO Matt Maloney sent a company-wide email condemning Donald Trump's "politics of hatred" and called for employees who disagreed to submit their resignation. The subsequent blowback he received induced him to quickly issue a "clarifying" statement, softening his former position.

Before the airing of the 2017 Emmy Awards, Stephen Colbert told Trump supporters "not to bother watching the awards show this year." Many agreed and chose not to watch.

Colbert's statement got me thinking about the plethora of award shows we see each year honoring music, television and movie moguls and performers. "What is it," I asked myself, "that induces Americans to watch with rapt attention as wealthy celebrities receive awards and accolades presented by other wealthy celebrities?" Maybe we somehow imagine ourselves in the role of those award recipients and that gives us a good feeling. Maybe not.

A recent celebrity near-disappointment for me was the case of screen actress, Jennifer Lawrence. I've enjoyed most of her films, especially *The Hunger Games*, *Silver Linings Playbook* and *American Hustle*, and so it disturbed me when I read that she believed the hurricanes in Texas and Florida were clearly signs of "Mother Nature's rage and wrath" at America for electing Donald Trump.

I had pretty much ignored some of her previous negative comments concerning Donald Trump. In a 2015 *Vogue* interview she said, "My view on the election is pretty cut-and-dried: If Donald Trump is president of the United States, it will be the end of the world." I didn't take that statement too seriously. After all, it was made a year before the election—even before Lawrence had expressed support for any particular candidate. Not only that, but I was looking forward to her next film.

The most recent quote, the one about "Mother Nature's rage," seemed pretty silly when I first heard it, until I realized that it came from a UK interview about her upcoming movie, *Mother!* The film is allegorical, with Biblical symbols and representation of man's environmental destruction of the Earth.

The blowback from the right that Jennifer Lawrence received in response to the statement about the hurricanes and the election of Donald Trump was fierce, but undeserved. She never said that the hurricanes were nature's punishment for electing Trump. This was pretty clear to anyone who watched the interview video or read the entire transcript as I did.

Not that anyone should care, but I felt better after determining that the criticism of Jennifer Lawrence—at least in this one important instance—was unfounded, and until she publicly says something else patently untrue or insulting about the president or his supporters, I'll continue to follow her career and support her films *(again, not that anyone should care!)*. Her latest film, *Mother! I*s an exception: while it received some critical acclaim, I am really not interested in seeing another film about man's environmental destruction of the planet.

But what of the others—the countless actors and performers who have been tragically struck down by this insidious affliction, Trump Derangement Syndrome? The unfortunate victims of this disorder don't understand that at least half the country is simply not interested in their political opinions.

Would I listen to medical advice from Madonna? Of course not, and if not, why would I be any more interested in what she has to say politically? And you might ask,

"Would you be interested in hearing some financial management advice from Johnny Depp?" I can say without equivocation, "Of course not!" So then, why would Johnny Depp's political opinions or politically-charged commentary hold any special interest for me?

More recently, nearly every late-night television host has joined in the cacophony of criticism of the president, relying on their writers to come up with clever, biting lines to deliver during their opening monologue. In fact, there is a long history of late-night hosts poking fun at administration officials, going back to Joan Rivers and Johnny Carson. In most cases, these hosts and many others that followed were "equal-opportunity" critics, taking humorous swipes at the Administration or Congress, no matter which political party was in power.

Now we are deluged with vicious attempts at humor directed at this president, his staff and supporters. To so many of us, the words of these hosts have become like the "clanging cymbal" that Paul speaks of in the New Testament.

But make no mistake, viewer ratings have risen steadily as more and more people tune in to validate the anger they've been holding inside for so long. Some wait in anticipation for the next outrageous insult to be hurled at the president, not unlike passing drivers in a queue, craning their necks to view the carnage of an accident. The sad thing is that most of the "jokes" aren't even funny.

Among the singers and celebrities of film and television, it is no secret that the majority have liberal views and support progressive political causes and candidates. We have to accept that most artists simply think that way—it's in their nature. And of this majority, most go about their business of entertainment without the compulsion to announce their political opinions to the world whenever a television camera is trained upon them. Perhaps they understand that they are the CEO of their personal realm with the responsibility for tending after their current film, music album or even their entire career. For these entertainers, I and countless others will continue to listen and watch as we respect that their personal political views may diverge from our own as much as the East is distant from the West.

There is, of course, that group of celebrities who seem driven to share their political views very loudly, publicly and negatively. Until modern medicine or psychiatry can come up with a cure for Trump Derangement Syndrome, I can only offer this simple advice to the singers and actors whose talents we someday hope to enjoy and appreciate once again:

SHUT UP AND SING*

SHUT UP AND ACT

As an additional word to those afflicted, I would add that if you must express yourself politically, go on a radio talk show, write a blog—or a book. That way, anyone who wishes to can easily tune-in, log-on or buy your book, and those that don't, won't be involuntarily subjected to your opinions. Acknowledge that you perpetrate a fraud on the public when you "bait" us with entertainment and then "switch" to a political diatribe.

---

*Shut Up & Sing is the title of a 2013 New York Times best-selling book by Laura Ingraham. The author acknowledges and cites Ms. Ingraham's prior use of this expression.

7.
Who Hacked the DNC?

THE CLAIM THAT IT WAS THE RUSSIAN Government that directed cyber-attacks on the Democratic National Committee Headquarters has supported the general theme of Russian interference in the U.S. electoral process.

As the story goes, in March 2016 John Podesta—then the chairman of Hillary Clinton's presidential campaign—responded to a phishing scam email that gave hackers access to one or more DNC servers. Some, including WikiLeaks Founder Julian Assange, have claimed that Podesta's email account was breached because his Gmail password was simply the word, "password," although there is no proof of that assertion. Such a scenario is

also questionable because I have heard—
but have not tried—anyone attempting to
create a new Gmail account and entering
"password" as the password will receive a
warning message rejecting the entry.

There is no question, however, that
Podesta's email account was compromised.
On July 22, 2016, just three days before the
start of the Democratic National
Convention, WikiLeaks released several
thousand emails originally resident on the
DNC server. Among them are messages that
clearly point to the DNC wholly supportive
of Hillary Clinton's candidacy for the
presidential nomination over that of Bernie
Sanders. It is this disclosure that led to the
DNC apology letter to Sanders and the
resignation of Chairperson, Debbie
Wasserman Schultz.

But the question of who is responsible
for the data breach and transmission of the
email messages to WikiLeaks remains open.
Julian Assange has on more than one
occasion denied that the Russian
Government (or a Russian "state party")
was the source of the messages. WikiLeaks
has a policy of non-disclosure regarding its
sources—understandable as disclosing
their identities would surely discourage
future data releases by others.

After the data breach, the DNC hired CrowdStrike, an Irvine California-based cybersecurity firm, to assess their systems and identify security deficiencies. Among CrowdStrike's findings was that Russian-supported hackers had compromised the server.

Some have questioned whether the claim of Russian involvement was unbiased considering that financial backers and owners of CrowdStrike have Democratic Party ties, and that such a finding would be welcomed by the DNC. CrowdStrike billings to the DNC have now exceeded $500,000.

CrowdStrike's determination was in part based upon the identification of a specific malware known as "X-Agent" on the DNC computers. Russian agencies, including the Russian Armed Forces Foreign Military Intelligence Agency—the GRU—have used this malware on previous occasions to penetrate U.S. Government networks at the White House and department of state. Critics claim that although X-Agent has Russian origins, it has been in use for years by many non-Russian surveillance agencies and independent hackers.

Beginning in August 2017, reports began to emerge that suggested that the prior assumptions regarding external hacking of DNC computers may have been all wrong. The reports claim that the data breach was likely a leak, not a hack. In essence, that it was an "inside job" undertaken by someone with access to the DNC server using a portable data storage device such as a high-capacity thumb drive. As evidence of this claim, it has been postulated that the high volume and apparent speed at which data were transferred would require a locally-executed download, and would not be possible from an external breach prosecuted through an internet connection.

The notion that the email leak may have been an "inside job" has revived interest in the much-debunked conspiracy theory surrounding the murder of DNC staffer, Seth Rich. Early in the morning of July 10, 2016, Rich was found near his Washington D.C. home with two gunshot wounds. He was rushed to a hospital where he later died. Police believe that the murder was the result of a botched robbery attempt—a botched attempt because Rich's wallet, watch and cell phone were not taken.

Public and media interest in the death of Seth Rich might have faded quickly if not for the WikiLeaks release of the stolen DNC emails less than two weeks later.

Conspiracy theorists on the right were quick to suggest that the murder of Seth Rich was a paid "hit" arranged by dark forces associated with elements within the Democratic Party as payback for stealing the emails that were later published by WikiLeaks. As a possible motive for the email leak, it was suggested that Rich may have been a Bernie Sanders supporter, unhappy with the DNC's treatment of his candidate.

During a YouTube interview on August 9, 2016, Julian Assange said, "Whistle-blowers go to significant efforts to get us material, and often very significant risks. A 27-year-old that works for the DNC was shot in the back—murdered—just two weeks ago, for unknown reasons, as he was walking down the street in Washington." When asked if Seth Rich was a source for WikiLeaks, Assange replied, "We don't comment on who our sources are." Later in the interview he said, "We are investigating to understand what happened in the situation with Seth Rich." Then several days later, Assange announced a $20,000 reward for information about the murder.

Liberals were quick to charge that the Seth Rich murder conspiracy theory was a baseless invention of the far-Right with support of the administration and designed to draw suspicion away from Russia as the source of the leaked emails. In a report that was retracted two days later, Fox News stated that the FBI had proof of an email exchange between Rich and WikiLeaks. The report from Fox included statements attributed to Fox contributor and investigator, Rod Wheeler. However, Wheeler filed a lawsuit against Fox on August 1, 2017, claiming that he never made the statements that were attributed to him—that they were invented by Fox. The lawsuit also claimed that Ed Bukowski, a Trump supporter, paid Wheeler to investigate Rich's death and that members of the White House staff were instrumental in furthering the false story.

As of this writing, the murder of Seth Rich remains an unsolved case, but the DC police still maintain their original finding that it was a murder committed during a botched robbery attempt. An NBC News report based on unnamed law enforcement sources stated that a police department examination of Rich's laptop computer contained no emails related or directed to WikiLeaks.

8.
Nothing Burger: Have it Your Way

IN HER RECENT MEMOIR, HILLARY Clinton claims that her use of a personal email server while she was secretary of state "was a dumb mistake, but an even dumber 'scandal'. It was like quicksand," she wrote, "the more you struggle, the deeper you sink."

Earlier, at a May 2017 conference in Rancho Palos Verdes, California, she said that the media treated the email story like "Pearl Harbor"—that it "was turned into the greatest scandal since Lord knows when. This was the biggest 'nothing-burger' ever."

I knew that many on the Left shared the opinion expressed by Mrs Clinton—an opinion perhaps best exemplified by a September 15, 2017, article in *The Atlantic*, by James Fallows. Fallows has been a long time apologist for the Democratic Party and its causes. He wrote the following in his article, "Why Hillary Clinton's Book Is Actually Worth Reading":

> NO SANE PERSON CAN BELIEVE THAT THE CONSEQUENCES OF LAST FALL'S ELECTION—FOR FOREIGN POLICY, FOR RACE RELATIONS, FOR THE ENVIRONMENT, FOR ANYTHING ELSE YOU'D LIKE TO NAME (FROM EITHER PARTY'S PERSPECTIVE)—SHOULD HAVE DEPENDED MORE THAN ABOUT 1 PERCENT ON WHAT HILLARY CLINTON DID WITH HER EMAILS. BUT THIS OBJECTIVELY SECOND- OR THIRD-TIER ISSUE CAME ACROSS THROUGH EVEN OUR BEST NEWS ORGANIZATIONS AS IF IT WERE THE *MAIN* THING WORTH KNOWING ABOUT ONE OF THE CANDIDATES.

Was it really just a "second- or third-tier" issue? It is an important enough question, certainly deserving a closer look.

Cheryl Mills was chief of staff to Hillary Clinton while Mrs Clinton served as secretary of state from 2009 to 2013. She provided sworn testimony during proceedings for a lawsuit brought by Judicial Watch. Judicial Watch is a conservative watchdog organization that seeks redress for alleged violations of the Freedom of Information Act.

Ms Mills stated that Mrs Clinton used a personal AT&T email account for official government business during the first three months after her appointment as secretary of state. It was the same email account that she had used during her tenure as Senator from the state of New York.

After an email server was set up in the Clinton home in Chappaqua, New York, Hillary began using the email address, hdr22@clintonemail.com, for all of her personal and work-related electronic correspondence. Mrs Clinton chose not to use a "state.gov" email account that would have been provided by the U.S. Government. Email accounts under the clintonmail.com domain were also set up for Cheryl Mills and Huma Abedin, a long-time staffer and aide to Hillary Clinton.

Critics of Mrs Clinton believe that she purposely chose a private server and email account so that her correspondence would never be open to Freedom of Information disclosure requests. It was charged that Hillary's intent was to hide potentially illegal or unethical activities, including "pay-for-play" corruption between the state department and international donors to the Clinton Foundation. In her sworn testimony, Cheryl Mills stated that the criticism was absolutely unfounded—that there was never an attempt to avoid Freedom of Information disclosure of state department business.

The disclosure of the existence of Mrs Clinton's email system first appeared publicly on March 2, 2015, in a front-page article in *The New York Times*. Days earlier, a House committee investigating the attack on the American Consulate in Benghazi had learned of Mrs Clinton's private email server. It was at a March 10th news conference at the United Nations that we heard Mrs Clinton explain that she set up her own email for "convenience." She said, "I opted for convenience to use my personal email account, which was allowed by the state department, because I thought it would be easier to carry just one device for my work and for my personal emails instead of two."

In July 2016 FBI Director James Comey testified that Mrs Clinton "used multiple devices during the four years of her term as secretary of state." With respect to the personal email account being "allowed" by the state department, there was no record of Mrs Clinton requesting nor obtaining approval to use private email on her private server for official business. According to state department regulations, official approval was required.

Perhaps what is most revealing about Mrs Clinton's real reason for using a homebrew server and private email is an ABC News video clip from a fundraiser for her year 2000 Senatorial campaign. In the video, she makes remarks about avoiding email for fear of leaving a paper trail. In speaking with a campaign donor during the luncheon, Mrs Clinton is heard to say, "As much as I've been investigated and all of that, you know, why would I—I don't even want—why would I ever want to do email? Can you imagine?"

After stepping down from her position as secretary of state, Mrs Clinton reported that she gave the state department more than 30,000 work-related emails from her private server and that she deleted nearly 32,000 emails that were considered personal. According to the FBI, the emails were deleted from the server just three weeks after the House Select Committee on Benghazi served Clinton with a subpoena to produce any and all emails related to its Benghazi investigation. When asked about the nature of the personal emails that were deleted, her office responded as follows:

> THESE WERE PRIVATE, PERSONAL MESSAGES, INCLUDING EMAILS ABOUT HER DAUGHTER'S WEDDING PLANS, HER MOTHER'S FUNERAL SERVICES, AND CONDOLENCE NOTES, AS WELL AS EMAILS ON FAMILY VACATIONS, YOGA ROUTINES, AND OTHER ITEMS ONE WOULD TYPICALLY FIND IN THEIR OWN EMAIL ACCOUNT, SUCH AS OFFERS FROM RETAILERS, SPAM, ETC.

Before closing the investigation, the FBI conducted a three-hour interview with Hillary Clinton. Notes of the interview released later revealed that Mrs Clinton was not placed under oath for the interview. Clinton told FBI investigators that she didn't understand that the "c" notation next to an email paragraph was used to designate the paragraph as one containing information that was classified as "confidential." She also said she didn't know the difference between different levels of classification, but "took them all seriously." She also stated that, while at the state department, she didn't recall ever receiving training on the handling of classified information.

In the FBI investigation of Mrs Clinton's private server and emails it was determined that although Mrs Clinton claimed that she never sent or received any classified information over her private email, that statement was untruthful. Director Comey stated that there was evidence that Mrs Clinton or her colleagues "were extremely careless in their handling of very sensitive, highly classified information."

Bryan Pagliano was a former state department staff member who had installed and maintained the Clinton's private email server at their home in Chappaqua, New York. On June 7, 2016, the Justice Department granted limited immunity to Pagliano for his cooperation with the FBI investigation concerning the Clinton's private email server. At a subsequent deposition for a lawsuit against the state department brought by Judicial Watch, Pagliano declined to answer any questions, invoking the Fifth Amendment at least 125 times. He also declined to appear and testify as requested by the House Oversight Committee on two separate occasions.

On September 22, 2016, members of the House Oversight and Government Reform

Committee voted to hold Pagliano in contempt for failing to appear. The vote passed without support from a single Democratic member of the committee.

In response to another Judicial Watch lawsuit, Hillary Clinton submitted formal written answers through her attorney about her use of the private email server. In twenty instances, her written answer was that she "did not recall" the requested information or related discussions. In one instance, the written answer from her lawyer was as follows:

> SECRETARY CLINTON STATES THAT SHE DOES NOT RECALL HAVING COMMUNICATIONS WITH BRYAN PAGLIANO CONCERNING OR RELATING TO THE MANAGEMENT, PRESERVATION, DELETION, OR DESTRUCTION OF ANY EMAILS IN HER CLINTONEMAIL.COM EMAIL ACCOUNT.

Yet some fifteen pages of documents published by Judicial Watch were the messages that Pagliano wrote directly to Mrs Clinton concerning her email system in March 2012.

AT THE CLOSE OF A HOUSE PANEL called two days after FBI Director James Comey recommended against prosecuting former Secretary of State Hillary Clinton for the email server scandal, Representative Trey Gowdy stated the following to the other members of the House panel and Director Comey:

> AND MY REAL FEAR IS THIS, WHAT THE CHAIRMAN TOUCHED UPON, THIS DOUBLE TRACK JUSTICE SYSTEM THAT IS RIGHTLY OR WRONGLY PERCEIVED IN THIS COUNTRY. THAT IF YOU ARE A PRIVATE IN THE ARMY AND EMAIL YOURSELF CLASSIFIED INFORMATION YOU WILL BE KICKED OUT. BUT IF YOU ARE HILLARY CLINTON, AND YOU SEEK A PROMOTION TO COMMANDER IN CHIEF, YOU WILL NOT BE. SO WHAT I HOPE YOU CAN DO TODAY IS HELP THE AVERAGE PERSON, THE REASONABLE PERSON YOU MADE REFERENCE TO, THE REASONABLE PERSON UNDERSTAND WHY SHE APPEARS TO BE TREATED DIFFERENTLY THAN THE REST OF US WOULD BE.

Trey Gowdy expressed the concern that James Comey's exoneration of Hillary Clinton was evidence of unfairness—of

unequal treatment under the law—
depending upon one's station in life.

It is doubtful that Representative Gowdy
had any real expectation that Comey could
make a "reasonable person understand
why" Mrs Clinton was given a pass for her
decisions and actions related to the careless
use of her private email. But despite the
chants of "Lock Her Up!" that we heard at
campaign rallies for Donald Trump during
the presidential campaign, I don't believe
that *most* Trump supporters and
independent voters wanted to see Hillary
Clinton sent to prison, any more than they
wanted to see her presiding in the West
Wing. Nonetheless, it seems clear that Mrs
Clinton's email problem became an
important addition to the accumulating list
of first-, second- and third-tier issues that
eventually caused her to lose the support of
so many voters.

9.
The Comey Conundrum

MORE THAN ANY OTHER SINGLE event of 2016, Hillary Clinton attributes her election loss on then-FBI Director James Comey's decision to notify Congress by letter just eleven days before the election that the email investigation was being reopened. She wrote in her memoir, ". . . if not for the dramatic intervention of the FBI director in the final days, I believe that in spite of everything, we would have won the White House."

James Comey was nominated to become director of the FBI by President Barack Obama and confirmed by the Senate on July 29, 2013. He replaced Robert Mueller, who had served as director since 2001.

With the serious concern over possible unauthorized disclosure of classified information, the FBI opened a criminal investigation in July 2015 into Hillary Clinton's use of a private email server while she was secretary of state. One year later, on July 5, 2016, Director Comey held a press conference where he called the behavior of Secretary Clinton and her top aides to be "extremely careless", but then concluded that "no reasonable prosecutor would bring such a case," effectively exonerating the secretary.

While it is the role of the FBI to make prosecutorial recommendations to the department of justice at the conclusion of an investigation, it is highly irregular to declare such recommendations publicly, and this case may have been unique in that regard. The declaration simply added to existing concerns about the case that arose a few days earlier over the "coincidental" meeting between Attorney General Loretta Lynch and Bill Clinton aboard her plane at the International Airport in Phoenix.

After a reporter happened to observe this encounter, and subsequent news reports criticized what appeared to be a blatant conflict of interest for the attorney general, Lynch announced that she would "fully accept" the recommendation of the FBI regarding the probe.

The day after James Comey's press conference, Attorney General Lynch confirmed that the investigation of Mrs Clinton and her aides was closed and that no criminal charges would be filed. She stated:

> LATE THIS AFTERNOON, I MET WITH FBI DIRECTOR JAMES COMEY AND CAREER PROSECUTORS AND AGENTS WHO CONDUCTED THE INVESTIGATION OF SECRETARY HILLARY CLINTON'S USE OF A PERSONAL EMAIL SYSTEM DURING HER TIME AS SECRETARY OF STATE. I RECEIVED AND ACCEPTED THEIR UNANIMOUS RECOMMENDATION THAT THE THOROUGH, YEAR-LONG INVESTIGATION BE CLOSED AND THAT NO CHARGES BE BROUGHT AGAINST ANY INDIVIDUALS WITHIN THE SCOPE OF THE INVESTIGATION.

While Hillary supporters cheered the decision and showered Director Comey with accolades for his uncompromised integrity and wisdom, most conservatives and Republican presidential candidate Trump cried foul. It is likely that Mrs Clinton and the entire DNC staff breathed a collective sigh of relief.

Over the next few weeks, Mrs Clinton was interviewed several times by mostly-supportive journalists, defending her email usage while acknowledging that she would do things differently if she could. During an interview with Anderson Cooper on August 24, 2016, Mrs Clinton is once again asked about her use of a private email account. She responds:

> I HAVE BEEN ASKED MANY, MANY QUESTIONS IN THE PAST YEAR ABOUT EMAILS, AND WHAT I HAVE LEARNED IS THAT WHEN I TRY TO EXPLAIN WHAT HAPPENED, IT CAN SOUND LIKE I AM TRYING TO EXCUSE WHAT I DID. AND THERE ARE NO EXCUSES. I WANT PEOPLE TO KNOW THAT THE DECISION TO HAVE A SINGLE EMAIL ACCOUNT WAS MINE. I TAKE RESPONSIBILITY FOR IT. I APOLOGIZE FOR IT. I WOULD CERTAINLY DO DIFFERENTLY IF I COULD. I BELIEVE THE PUBLIC WILL BE AND IS CONSIDERING MY FULL RECORD AND EXPERIENCE AS THEY CONSIDER THEIR CHOICE FOR PRESIDENT.

The opinions held by Progressives and Conservatives regarding James Comey were reversed suddenly when on October 28, 2016, the FBI director sent a letter notifying Congress that the Clinton email investigation had been reopened. He wrote:

IN CONNECTION WITH AN UNRELATED CASE, THE FBI HAS LEARNED OF THE EXISTENCE OF EMAILS THAT APPEAR TO BE PERTINENT TO THE INVESTIGATION. I AM WRITING TO INFORM YOU THAT THE INVESTIGATIVE TEAM BRIEFED ME ON THIS YESTERDAY, AND I AGREED THAT THE FBI SHOULD TAKE APPROPRIATE INVESTIGATIVE STEPS DESIGNED TO ALLOW INVESTIGATORS TO REVIEW THESE EMAILS TO DETERMINE WHETHER THEY CONTAIN CLASSIFIED INFORMATION, AS WELL AS TO ASSESS THEIR IMPORTANCE TO OUR INVESTIGATION.

ALTHOUGH THE FBI CANNOT YET ASSESS WHETHER OR NOT THIS MATERIAL MAY BE SIGNIFICANT, AND I CANNOT PREDICT HOW LONG IT WILL TAKE US TO COMPLETE THIS ADDITIONAL WORK, I BELIEVE IT IS IMPORTANT TO UPDATE YOUR COMMITTEES ABOUT OUR EFFORTS IN LIGHT OF MY PREVIOUS TESTIMONY.

The "unrelated case" was the investigation of former Congressman Anthony Weiner. FBI agents examining Weiner's computer discovered emails between Hillary Clinton and Weiner's wife, Huma Abedin, who was deputy chief of staff to the secretary at that time.

Comey came under fire by many on the left. Senator Dianne Feinstein, leading Democrat on the Senate Intelligence Committee, said that the FBI's vague announcement "played right into the political campaign of Donald Trump" and added, "The FBI has a history of extreme caution near Election Day so as not to influence the results. Today's break from that tradition is appalling." John Podesta, chairman of Clinton's presidential campaign, stated:

IT IS EXTRAORDINARY THAT WE WOULD SEE SOMETHING LIKE THIS JUST 11 DAYS OUT FROM A PRESIDENTIAL ELECTION. THE DIRECTOR OWES IT TO THE AMERICAN PEOPLE TO IMMEDIATELY PROVIDE THE FULL DETAILS OF WHAT HE IS NOW EXAMINING. WE ARE CONFIDENT THIS WILL NOT PRODUCE ANY CONCLUSIONS DIFFERENT FROM THE ONE THE FBI REACHED IN JULY.

In a *Wall Street Journal* article published two days later, it was reported that Federal agents were preparing to sift through some 650,000 emails found on Weiner's laptop. There may have been thousands sent to or from the private server account that Mrs Clinton used while she was secretary of state. The *Journal* article stated that "the review will take weeks at a minimum."

It was somewhat surprising, then, when just eight days later, in a second letter from James Comey to Congress that the FBI Director wrote, "Based on our review, we have not changed our conclusions that we expressed in July." The net result was that after opening two Clinton email investigations and issuing exonerations after each, Director Comey was broadly criticized for his actions from both the Right and the Left. Candidate Trump questioned the ability of the FBI to review and clear 650,000 emails in just eight days. Dianne Feinstein criticized both the FBI reopening the investigation and the review. She said:

> TODAY'S LETTER MAKES DIRECTOR COMEY'S ACTIONS NINE DAYS AGO EVEN MORE TROUBLING. THERE'S NO DOUBT THAT IT CREATED A FALSE IMPRESSION ABOUT THE NATURE OF THE AGENCY'S INQUIRY. THE JUSTICE DEPARTMENT

NEEDS TO TAKE A LOOK AT ITS PROCEDURES TO PREVENT SIMILAR ACTIONS THAT COULD INFLUENCE FUTURE ELECTIONS.

After the first FBI investigation of the Clinton private email server and handling of classified information, it seemed curious to me that agents would spend a whole year in investigation, uncover several serious violations, and then fail to bring charges against anyone on grounds that there was no "intent" to break the law. After the reopening of the investigation in October 2016 and closing it again after only eight days, I could only utter what has become the classic Scooby-Doo response, *"Huh?"*

It seemed worthwhile to look into Director Comey's background in hopes of identifying events or associations that may have influenced the decisions he made in the Clinton email affair. Items to consider were the following:

- Comey was a registered Republican until 2016; then an Independent.

- In May 2009 some Obama White House officials pushed for Comey's inclusion on a short list of names to replace retiring Justice David Souter on the U.S. Supreme Court.

- He became Director of the FBI after being nominated by Barack Obama in 2013; he reported to Attorney General, Loretta Lynch.

- Despite unproven claims by some right-wing sources, James Comey was never a member of the board of the Clinton Foundation, although he has been on the board of directors of at least two corporations that have made donations to the Clinton Foundation.

- Comey contributed to John McCain's 2008 presidential campaign, Mitt Romney's 2012 presidential primary campaign and general election, and to Susan Brooks, a Republican candidate for Congress in 2012. No other records of his recent contributions to political campaigns could be found.

While the listed items are somewhat interesting, it is doubtful that anything in the previous list was a motivating factor for Director Comey in the Clinton email case. Of course, one would expect no less of any official in what should be a non-partisan position.

President Obama's Justice Department may have preferred to ignore the potential violations   associated   with   the clintonmail.com private server, but once the mishandling of classified information was publicly disclosed in 2015, Attorney General Loretta Lynch had no choice but to order an FBI investigation to proceed. But that is not to say that the Justice Department couldn't—or wouldn't—try to influence the outcome of the investigation. It was in the interest of the Obama Administration that damage to Hillary Clinton's presidential bid be minimized, and that ultimate result was at least partially achieved.

During Congressional testimony on June 8, 2017, former-Director Comey said, referring to Lynch, "I wanted to know, was she going to authorize us to confirm we had an investigation, and she said, 'Yes, but don't call it that, call it a matter,'" Comey added. "And I said, 'Why would I do that?' And she said, 'Just call it a matter.'"

In September 2017, reports began to emerge that Comey had composed a draft of the Clinton exoneration letter as much as two months before interviewing key witnesses and completing the investigation. Senate judiciary committee members Grassley and Graham wrote to FBI Director Christopher Wray seeking more information:

CONCLUSION FIRST, FACT-GATHERING SECOND — THAT'S NO WAY TO RUN AN INVESTIGATION. THE FBI SHOULD BE HELD TO A HIGHER STANDARD THAN THAT, ESPECIALLY IN A MATTER OF SUCH GREAT PUBLIC INTEREST AND CONTROVERSY.

When the additional Clinton emails were found during the FBI Anthony Weiner investigation, Comey was faced with two politically-sensitive courses of action: He could (1) reopen the case, which would surely cause some voters to drop their support for Mrs Clinton and potentially throw the election to Mr Trump, or (2) proceed with the new investigation without disclosing that it was underway with the understanding that the outcome might not be known until after Election Day. With Mrs Clinton leading in the polls, the second course of action would no doubt result in charges that the FBI was "in the tank" for Mrs Clinton— shielding her campaign from more bad news until the election was decided.

In the end, Director Comey chose the first course of action, but with a twist that may have been ordered by the AG or her boss in the Oval Office. The Director needed only to complete three simple steps: (1) announce the reopening of the email investigation, (2) review all of the pertinent emails quickly by working the agents diligently—harder than they have ever worked before—and (3) announce before election day that the FBI had not changed its earlier conclusion. That is, that neither Mrs Clinton nor members of her staff should face charges over mishandling of classified information.

Another—perhaps overriding—factor in Comey's decision arose out of rumors that the FBI agents who discovered the additional emails during the investigation of Anthony Weiner had threatened to resign and disclose the discovery if Comey had delayed or refused to reopen the email investigation. As of this writing, those rumors have never been substantiated.

This was a no-win situation for the former FBI director. He had alienated important factions within both political parties. Within five months he would lose his job—although it is unlikely that he was ever "comfortable" in the role of FBI director after the inauguration of Donald Trump.

Fortunately for the former director, we learned in August 2017 that he had signed a "multi-million dollar" book deal with publisher, Flat Iron Books. Flat Iron President Bob Miller stated that Director Comey "will give us unprecedented entry into the corridors of power, and a remarkable lesson in leadership itself." Comey's book, *A Higher Loyalty: Truth, Lies, and Leadership*, was published in 2018.

10.
A True Grassroots Candidate

A GRASSROOTS MOVEMENT IS DEFINED as one that uses the people in a given district—local, regional or national—as the basis for a political or economic movement. Third-party and independent candidates for political office are often local or regional personalities who grow in popularity through word-of-mouth and other people-to-people interactions.

Sometimes it is difficult to determine when a candidate has risen to any level of prominence as the result of a true grassroots movement or maybe a false one, intended to fool potential supporters into joining the movement. The term "astroturfing"—derived from the name of the well-known artificial grass product, AstroTurf® (a registered trademark)—has been used to describe the act of disguising a political campaign backed by powerful financial interests or political forces to appear as though it has grown organically from some native grassroots-like appeal.

Looking at the slate of presidential candidates running in advance of the 2016 election, we find several major party candidates as well as third-party hopefuls. 2016 third-party presidential candidates included the following:

- Gary Johnson, the former Republican governor of New Mexico, ran as the Libertarian Party candidate. His running mate was William Weld, the former governor of Massachusetts. They received a credible 3.3% of the total popular vote in 2016.

- Jill Stein, a physician from Massachusetts, was the Green Party candidate and ended up with 1.1% of the popular vote.

- Ewan McMullin is a former CIA operations officer and has held important Republican Party staff positions in the House of Representatives. He announced his candidacy for president on August 8, 2016, calling himself a conservative alternative to Republican nominee Donald Trump. McMullin ran as an independent and garnered just 0.5% of the popular vote in 2016.

Both Johnson and Stein had run for president in 2012 under their same 2016 party affiliations. As an interesting aside, the Marijuana Policy Project voter guide gave both Johnson and Stein ratings of A+ in 2016, resulting in the cynical, tongue-in-cheek declaration that they each "ran a popular grassroots campaign."

By the time that individuals seeking the presidential nomination from one of the two national parties become viable enough to participate in party-sponsored debates, it is not always clear how they got there. Did they enjoy true grassroots popularity? A clue can be found by examining their incoming donation records.

According to a *Wall Street Journal* article dated October 28, 2015, only Bernie Sanders, Ben Carson and Rand Paul among national party candidates received at least 50% of their donation totals from individual donor contributions of $200 or less, excluding donations to super PACs. The data presented included donations received through September 30, 2015.

As reported in the article, 77% of total donations to the Bernie Sanders campaign came from individual donations of $200 or less—the highest percentage among all national party candidates. Before withdrawing from the race on July 12, 2016, Sanders' grassroots campaign was the recipient of more than 7 million individual contributions averaging just $27 each. Rand Paul had dropped out of the race for the Republican nomination some five months earlier, on February 3, while Ben Carson announced his withdrawal a month after that.

In the early days of the campaign, it was rumored that Massachusetts Senator Elizabeth Warren might enter the race for the Democratic nomination. There was much excitement expressed over the potential strength of her candidacy considering her perceived grassroots appeal with voters. But when the liberal groups MoveOn.org and Democracy for America pledged more than $1.2 million to begin "organizing" in a few states on Warren's behalf, it is likely that many began to wonder if her apparent grassroots appeal was really only "astroturf."

BERNIE SANDERS DID NOT BECOME THE Democratic nominee for the 2016 presidential election, but he came close. I suspect there were occasions prior to Sanders' withdrawal that Mrs Clinton was fearful that history might repeat itself—that just as in 2008 when Barack Obama snatched the nomination to which she felt entitled, that Bernie Sanders might do the same.

Bernie Sanders was born and raised in Brooklyn, New York, and graduated from the University of Chicago in 1964 with a degree in political science. While at the university, Sanders joined the youth affiliate of the Socialist Party of America and was active in the Civil Rights Movement, participating in sit-ins and anti-war demonstrations. His application for conscientious objector status during the Vietnam War was under review for an extended period of time. It has been reported that when Sanders finally received the news that his application had been rejected, he was beyond the draft board's maximum eligibility age.

Bernie returned to New York City after graduation, working a variety of jobs, and then moved to Vermont in 1968. He began his political career as the Liberty Union

Party candidate for governor of Vermont in 1972 and 1976. The Liberty Union Party was a Socialist-oriented activist group affiliated with other far-Left organizations including the Socialist Party USA, the People's Party and Workers World Party. He lost both gubernatorial elections as well as his bids to run for the U.S Senate in 1972 and 1974.

Finally, running as an independent in 1981, he won the mayoral race for the City of Burlington, Vermont, with a margin of ten votes and went on to be reelected three times. He was elected to Congress in 1990 and served eight terms in the House of Representatives before becoming a U.S. Senator from Vermont in 2006. Considering his multiple terms in both the House of Representatives and the Senate, Bernie Sanders has become the longest serving independent in U.S. congressional history.

His reelection bids have been won by large margins by promoting popular Left-wing causes including income inequality, global warming, LGBT rights and universal healthcare. He opposed U.S. involvement in the First Gulf War and the invasion of Iraq as well as government surveillance initiatives like the Patriot Act and wide-reaching NSA special programs that have impacted individual privacy rights.

ON MAY 26, 2015, BERNIE SANDERS launched his campaign to seek the Democratic Party nomination for president. At an address to students at Liberty University in September 2015, Sanders explained why he was running as a Democrat, participating in Democratic primaries, instead of as an independent candidate:

> IF WE WERE SERIOUS ABOUT WINNING THIS ELECTION, WHICH IS ALWAYS MY INTENTION FROM DAY ONE, I THOUGHT WE COULD AND I HOPE THAT WE WILL. I HAD TO DO IT WITHIN THE DEMOCRATIC PRIMARY CAUCUS PROCESS.

> WHAT I DID NOT WANT TO DO IS RUN AS A THIRD PARTY CANDIDATE, TAKE VOTES AWAY FROM THE DEMOCRATIC CANDIDATE AND HELP ELECT SOME RIGHT-WING REPUBLICAN. I DID NOT WANT RESPONSIBILITY FOR THAT. SO WHAT I SAID AT THE BEGINNING OF THE CAMPAIGN IS THAT I WAS NOT GOING TO RUN AS AN INDEPENDENT. AND I SAY IT NOW, THAT IF I DO NOT WIN THIS PROCESS I WILL NOT RUN AS AN INDEPENDENT.

Sanders was enjoying some success at that point in time. The CBS Battleground Tracker poll showed Sanders with a comfortable lead over Hillary Clinton in both Iowa and New Hampshire, although Clinton was ahead in South Carolina. Bernie was able to consistently draw larger crowds at many of his rallies. In late January 2016, both candidates held separate events in Dubuque, Iowa, on the same day. Crowd size for Hillary was 450 and 1,300 for Bernie. In the end, Mrs Clinton managed to eke out a victory over Sanders in the Iowa primary, beating him by just 0.2 percentage points.

There was a sense of excitement in the Sanders campaign—palpable at his rallies—but there were also concerns. As one Sanders supporter wrote, "My hope is that this is the beginning, and not just a flash-in-the pan presidential campaign around one very adorable 74-year-old socialist."

In a March 28, 2016, NMPolitics.net article by Heath Haussamen, the author tells the story of a grassroots group called "Las Cruces for BERNIE" started by an exuberant Sanders supporter, one Claudia Piper. Because the group was not formally affiliated with Sanders' campaign, it was not permitted to use any part of the candidate's name in its own name, so the "BERNIE" in "Las Cruces for BERNIE" was an acronym for "Being Extremely Realistic Now In Elections."

Nonetheless, the group raised funds and made bumper stickers, buttons and T-shirts supporting Sanders. In the article, author Haussamen quotes Piper, who in 1960 was a journalism student at the University of Colorado and not quite old enough to vote in the Kennedy v. Nixon presidential election of that year. She states:

> BERNIE ENGAGES YOUNG PEOPLE THE WAY KENNEDY ENGAGED MY GENERATION.

> WHAT'S HAPPENING IN LAS CRUCES IS HAPPENING THROUGHOUT THE STATE AND ACROSS THE NATION. THESE GROUPS, WITH THEIR LOCAL ACTIONS AND MEDIA OUTREACH, ARE THE ONLY REASONS THE BERNIE CAMPAIGN HAS BEEN ABLE TO BREAK THROUGH THE CORPORATE MEDIA BLACKOUT.

> I HAVE ADMIRED BERNIE FOR MANY, MANY YEARS BECAUSE HE SEEMED THE MOST HONEST, PROGRESSIVE, AND PRINCIPLED MEMBER OF CONGRESS. I

GOT SO EXCITED LAST SPRING AFTER HEARING HIS SPEECHES. 'THIS GUY IS THE REAL DEAL,' I THOUGHT. I IMMEDIATELY LIKED HIS PLATFORM, AND MY ADMIRATION FOR HIS INTEGRITY AND DETERMINATION CONTINUES TO SURGE.

But despite the energy and dedication of the Las Cruces for BERNIE group, Hillary Clinton managed a 3% margin of victory over Bernie Sanders in the New Mexico Democratic primary election on June 7, 2016. The pledged delegate split was 18 for Clinton and 16 for Sanders, but Hillary had a "bonus" of nine additional nominally unpledged delegates—presumably these were Democratic Party superdelegates.

Among pledged delegates to the Democratic National Convention, Hillary Clinton beat Bernie Sanders by 359 delegates. But it was her overwhelming margin in superdelegates—as detailed previously in Chapter 2—that gave her enough delegates to exceed the 2,383 needed to win the nomination.

From early in the race, Sanders supporters complained that the DNC had stacked the deck in Hillary's favor in several ways, including arranging earlier-than-usual primary dates for states that Mrs Clinton was expected to win as well as some important debate details that were biased in Hillary's favor. Sanders was disadvantaged by both the limited number of debates and the fact that they were scheduled on weekends during late hours of the evening.

Finally, in May 2016, the Clinton campaign announced that it would not participate in a California debate that was to be co-sponsored by Fox News and the *San Francisco Chronicle*. Sanders had previously accepted the network's invitation to debate, and upon learning that Mrs Clinton would not participate, Sanders remarked, "I am disappointed but not surprised by Secretary Clinton's unwillingness to debate before the largest and most important primary in the presidential nominating process." In further response to the news, Sanders campaign manager Jeff Weaver said:

> MORE THAN HALF WAY THROUGH THE MONTH OF MAY, WE HOPE SECRETARY CLINTON WILL SOON MAKE GOOD ON HER CAMPAIGN'S COMMITMENT AND AGREE TO A TIME AND PLACE FOR A DEBATE. THERE ARE ISSUES OF ENORMOUS IMPORTANCE FACING THE PEOPLE OF CALIFORNIA AND OUR NATION AND THE PEOPLE OF OUR LARGEST STATE DESERVE TO HEAR THE DEMOCRATIC CANDIDATES OPINIONS.

Although we didn't know it at the time, it was subsequently disclosed in the hacked (or stolen) DNC emails released by WikiLeaks that Donna Brazile had leaked town hall meeting and primary debate questions to the Clinton campaign before the events took place. Ms Brazile, a political analyst for CNN at the time, resigned from the network on October 14, 2016, in the face of criticism for her actions.

We wonder how the results of the 2016 Democratic National Convention may have been impacted if the WikiLeaks disclosure regarding Donna Brazile and the debate questions had occurred *before* the last series of state caucuses and primary elections were held.

MONTHS AFTER THE ELECTION AND more than a year after the Democratic National Convention, Bernie Sanders continues to be a popular political figure. A March 2017 Fox News poll showed Sanders with a 61% approval rating, the highest of all politicians included in the poll, with Donald Trump at 43%. Similar results were reported in other national polls, including the April 2017 Harvard-Harris Poll.

Conservatives argue that Sanders' popularity is greatest among the youngest class of voters—especially millennials—because Sanders' socialist programs like free higher education and universal health care rank high on their list of priorities.

A few days after suspending his own 2020 campaign for president, Bernie Sanders formally endorsed former Vice President Joe Biden for president on April 13, 2020.

11.
What Difference Does It Make?

ON SEPTEMBER 11, 2012, THE U.S. diplomatic compound in Benghazi, Libya, was attacked resulting in the deaths of Chris Stevens, U.S. ambassador to Libya, and Sean Smith, a foreign service IT officer. Seven hours later the CIA Annex, about one mile from the diplomatic compound, came under gunfire and a mortar attack that killed two CIA contractor personnel, Tyrone Woods and Glen Doherty. Doherty had flown in from Tripoli, some 600 miles away, with a contingent of reinforcements after learning of the attack on the diplomatic compound. Both Doherty and Woods were former Navy SEALs.

Defense Secretary Leon Panetta learned of the first attack within an hour, and Secretary of State Hillary Clinton was soon in contact with CIA Director David Petraeus. An unarmed surveillance drone had already been redirected to the airspace above Benghazi, providing video updates of the scene on the ground. The dead and injured were flown out of the city the next day, and when the situation in Benghazi was stabilized, all of the diplomatic staff were moved to the capital in Tripoli.

Within 24 hours U.S. officials were describing the attacks as growing out of a spontaneous protest triggered by a recently released anti-Muslim video. The video, *Innocence of Muslims*, was also blamed for earlier anti-U.S. demonstrations in Egypt.

The Obama Administration wasted no time in spreading the story. It has been reported that the CIA was the source of the talking points document distributed to Administration staff and any other personnel who might be asked about what may have precipitated the attacks.

On September 16, the U.S. Ambassador to the U.N. Susan Rice appeared on five major Sunday television news programs about the Benghazi incident, blaming the video at each appearance for precipitating the carnage. The following is her statement from one of those news programs:

BASED ON THE BEST INFORMATION WE HAVE TO DATE, WHAT OUR ASSESSMENT IS AS OF THE PRESENT IS IN FACT WHAT BEGAN SPONTANEOUSLY IN BENGHAZI AS A REACTION TO WHAT HAD TRANSPIRED SOME HOURS EARLIER IN CAIRO WHERE, OF COURSE, AS YOU KNOW, THERE WAS A VIOLENT PROTEST OUTSIDE OF OUR EMBASSY—SPARKED BY THIS HATEFUL VIDEO. BUT SOON AFTER THAT SPONTANEOUS PROTEST BEGAN OUTSIDE OF OUR CONSULATE IN BENGHAZI, WE BELIEVE THAT IT LOOKS LIKE EXTREMIST ELEMENTS, INDIVIDUALS, JOINED IN THAT— IN THAT EFFORT WITH HEAVY WEAPONS OF THE SORT THAT ARE, UNFORTUNATELY, READILY NOW AVAILABLE IN LIBYA POST-REVOLUTION.

Secretary Clinton and President Obama met with families of the Benghazi victims at Joint Base Andrews in Maryland on September 14, 2012. Four teams of seven Marines carried the flag-draped caskets of the fallen off a C-17 transport plane. According to family members of two of the victims, Hillary told them, "We are going to have the film maker arrested who was responsible." Family members of the other two victims claimed that Mrs Clinton made no mention of the video to them. Mrs Clinton has denied that she ever blamed the video when meeting with the families of those Americans killed in Benghazi. In her 2014 book, *Hard Choices*, Mrs Clinton defended her earlier statements about the video and the cause of the Benghazi attacks. She wrote:

I MYSELF WENT BACK AND FORTH ON WHAT LIKELY HAPPENED, WHO DID IT, AND WHAT MIX OF FACTORS- LIKE THE VIDEO- PLAYED A PART. BUT IT WAS UNQUESTIONABLY INCITING THE REGION AND TRIGGERING PROTESTS ALL OVER, SO IT WOULD HAVE BEEN STRANGE NOT TO CONSIDER, AS DAYS OF PROTESTS UNFOLDED, THAT IT MIGHT HAVE HAD THE SAME EFFECT HERE, TOO. THAT'S JUST COMMON SENSE. LATER INVESTIGATION AND REPORTING CONFIRMED THAT THE VIDEO WAS INDEED A FACTOR. ALL WE KNEW AT THAT TIME WITH COMPLETE CERTAINTY WAS THAT AMERICANS HAD BEEN KILLED AND OTHERS WERE STILL IN DANGER.

And yet in one of the state department emails released to the House Select

Committee on Benghazi, Mrs Clinton writes the following to her daughter Chelsea just after learning of the attack:

> TWO OF OUR OFFICERS WERE KILLED IN BENGHAZI BY AN AL QAEDA-LIKE GROUP: THE AMBASSADOR, WHOM I HANDPICKED AND A YOUNG COMMUNICATIONS OFFICER ON TEMPORARY DUTY W/ A WIFE AND TWO SMALL CHILDREN. VERY HARD DAY AND I FEAR MORE OF THE SAME TOMORROW.

Hillary spoke by phone with the Egyptian Foreign Minister after the story condemning the video for the attack began to circulate. In the email she sent documenting her phone conversation she wrote:

> WE KNOW THAT THE ATTACK IN LIBYA HAD NOTHING TO DO WITH THE FILM. IT WAS A PLANNED ATTACK—NOT A PROTEST. . . . BASED ON THE INFORMATION WE SAW TODAY WE BELIEVE THE GROUP THAT CLAIMED RESPONSIBILITY FOR THIS WAS AFFILIATED WITH AL QAEDA.

Conservatives have charged that the story of outrage over an anti-Muslim video as the cause of the Benghazi attacks was a fabrication of the Obama Administration, created out of a concern that the incident and the administration's weak response to it might derail the president's reelection bid. The election was less than two months away, and the successful attack against an American facility overseas was contrary to the president's narrative that "Osama bin Laden is dead and al Qaeda is on the run." On the fourth anniversary of the attack on Benghazi, Gregory Hicks, former career state department employee stated in a Fox News interview:

CANDIDATE CLINTON AND HER CAMPAIGN POINT TO HER RECORD AS SECRETARY OF STATE AS A POSITIVE QUALIFICATION FOR THE PRESIDENCY. HOWEVER, THE RECORD SHOWS THAT SECRETARY CLINTON PERSUADED THE PRESIDENT TO OVERTHROW QADDAFI AND ADVOCATED MAINTAINING A DIPLOMATIC PRESENCE IN BENGHAZI AFTER THE LIBYAN REVOLUTION. AND THEN SHE ABANDONED HER DIPLOMATS BY IGNORING HER SECURITY OBLIGATIONS. SHE SENT AMBASSADOR STEVENS TO BENGHAZI DURING THE 2011 REVOLUTION AND THEN INDUCED HIM TO RETURN IN THE FIRST FEW MONTHS OF HIS TENURE, WHICH ACCOUNTED FOR HIS SEPTEMBER VISIT THERE.

. . . . EITHER SHE COULD NOT CORRELATE THE INCREASED TEMPO OF ATTACKS IN LIBYA WITH THE SAFETY OF OUR DIPLOMATS, DEMONSTRATING FATAL INCOMPETENCE, OR SHE WAS GROSSLY NEGLIGENT.

IF MRS CLINTON WAS UNABLE TO FULFILL HER SECURITY OBLIGATIONS TO THE FEDERAL EMPLOYEES SHE WAS LEGALLY OBLIGATED TO PROTECT AS SECRETARY OF STATE, HOW CAN WE TRUST HER WITH THE SECURITY OF OUR ENTIRE COUNTRY?

I WON'T.

And what of the filmmaker, the creator of the video, *Innocence of Muslims*, that caused such controversy? Nakoula Basseley Nakoula is an Egyptian-born Coptic Christian immigrant who operated one or more gas stations in Southern California in the early 1990s. Serious financial difficulties led to the filing of liens against his business for unpaid taxes and penalties and later for failing to meet the terms of a bankruptcy arrangement. The liens filed against Nakoula eventually totaled several hundred thousand dollars.

In 1997 he was arrested and pleaded guilty to a charge of intent to manufacture methamphetamine. After his release from Los Angeles County jail, he was arrested again for a probation violation and served more jail time. In 2010 he was arrested for participation in a check-kiting bank fraud scheme—eventually to be released on probation in 2011.

Nakoula was questioned by Federal authorities on September 15, 2012, just four days after the Benghazi attack. He was arrested on September 27 and charged with eight counts of probation violation. Federal prosecutors determined that the terms of Nakoula's probation restricted his use of the internet—terms which he violated when he posted the video on YouTube.

Nakoula was released from custody in August 2013 to serve the balance of his term at a homeless shelter in Buena Park, California, sponsored by Pastor Wiley Drake of the First Southern Baptist Church. Nakoula claimed that he wrote the script for the video while in prison, and that his wife's family in Egypt had given him more than $50,000 that he used to cover the cost of producing the video. It is not known if the family was aware of his intended use for the funds.

At last report, according to a Wikipedia article, Nakoula was living at a Los Angeles homeless shelter, working part-time at a pizza parlor. His plans for the future included writing a book about his ordeal.

12.
Who Was That Masked Man?

O N SEPTEMBER 20, 2017, IT WAS disclosed in a Fox News report that Samantha Power, former U.S. ambassador to the United Nations under the Obama Administration, had made more than 260 requests in the previous year to unmask the identities of Americans caught up in routine surveillance of foreign officials. The "Foreign Intelligence Surveillance Act," or FISA, allows U.S. surveillance agencies to monitor communications between U.S. citizens and foreign nationals. However, the actual identity of the U.S. citizen may not be disclosed to other agencies or personnel unless officials follow proper procedures to make sure that identification of the individual is being done for a demonstrably acceptable reason.

As an example, if the communications of a foreign prime minister are under surveillance and that person telephones Senator Smith in the U.S., the Senator's name in the transcript of the conversation would be replaced with an alias such as "U.S. Person #1," effectively concealing or "masking" his identity. The transcript might then be made available to an authorized official with a legitimate interest in the subject matter, but in order to learn the actual identity of U.S. Person #1, the official is *supposed to* submit a good reason why the actual name should be revealed. Or maybe not.

The Trump Administration has charged that former officials in the Obama administration, including Samantha Power and Susan Rice, had illegally requested the unmasking of some Trump transition team officials for political reasons. The purpose of the unmasking, presumably, was to obtain and disclose evidence that supports the claim of Russian collusion with Trump officials prior to the election.

During a September 22, 2017, radio program, political commentator and author Mark Steyn explained why unmasking became commonplace during the last days of the Obama administration:

THERE HAS BEEN LITTLE EVIDENCE OF INTERNATIONAL INTERFERENCE IN THE ELECTION, BUT THERE'S PLENTY OF EVIDENCE OF DOMESTIC INTERFERENCE: EAVESDROPPING ON FOREIGN CITIZENS FOR THE EXPRESS PURPOSE OF LISTENING TO MEMBERS OF THE TRUMP CAMPAIGN AND ADMINISTRATION IN HOPES OF UNDERMINING AND OVERTHROWING IT.

NO ONE CARED WHAT SHEIKH MOHAMMED BIN ZAYED AL NAHYAN FROM THE UAE WAS SAYING—THEY WANTED TO HEAR WHAT THE TRUMP REPRESENTATIVE WAS SAYING AND PLANNING ON THE OTHER END OF THE LINE. THE RUSSIA INVESTIGATION WAS A PRETEXT FOR DOMESTIC INTERFERENCE AIMED AT CANDIDATE AND PRESIDENT TRUMP.

Unnamed sources behind the Fox News report stated that the unmasking requests continued up to the day of President Trump's inauguration.

The controversy over probable illegal unmasking of Trump team members arose earlier from a July 2017 letter from Intelligence Committee Chairman Devin Nunes. In the letter to Dan Coats, the director of national intelligence, Nunes questioned why nearly every unmasking request was based upon "boilerplate" justification, without specific details as to why the information was needed. He also stated in the letter:

WE HAVE FOUND EVIDENCE THAT CURRENT AND FORMER GOVERNMENT OFFICIALS HAD EASY ACCESS TO U.S. PERSON INFORMATION AND THAT IT IS POSSIBLE THAT THEY USED THIS INFORMATION TO ACHIEVE PARTISAN POLITICAL PURPOSES, INCLUDING THE SELECTIVE, ANONYMOUS LEAKING OF SUCH INFORMATION.

The letter did not mention former Ambassador Samantha Power by name, but referred to that person simply as "one official":

THE COMMITTEE HAS LEARNED THAT ONE OFFICIAL, WHOSE POSITION HAD NO APPARENT INTELLIGENCE RELATED FUNCTION, MADE HUNDREDS OF UNMASKING REQUESTS DURING THE FINAL YEAR OF THE OBAMA ADMINISTRATION,

In January 2017, a *Washington Post* article developed from a "senior U.S. government official" reported that retired

General Michael Flynn had been in contact with the Russian ambassador to the U.S., Sergey Kislyak, on multiple occasions. Flynn had worked in the Trump campaign and served as his national security adviser for a short time until it was reported that he had lied to Vice President Pence regarding the extent and details of his conversations with Kislyak.

After Flynn tendered his resignation, it was reported that he had previously received large payments from Russian companies and individuals. Flynn offered to testify to Congress only if granted immunity from prosecution.

It was later determined that Flynn's name was among those individuals unmasked by an unnamed Obama administration official. Conservative critics complained that the real story surrounding the Flynn affair was the unmasking of Flynn and leaking his name to the media, an abuse of power and illegal disclosure of classified information. It was charged that for political purposes, Obama's national security advisor, Susan Rice, or some other high-level Obama official was seeking to correlate sensitive conversations obtained through surveillance activities with the identities of members on Trump's transition team. Rice denied the accusation during an MSNBC interview with Andrea Mitchell. "The allegation is that, somehow, Obama administration officials utilized intelligence for political purposes. That's absolutely false," Rice said. In support of Ms Rice's response, former CIA analyst Nada Bakos said the following:

> IN A SITUATION WHERE THERE'S INCIDENTAL COLLECTION AND IT APPEARS THAT THEY'RE DISCUSSING U.S. INCOMING OR CURRENT OFFICIALS, IT WOULD NOT BE UNUSUAL FOR A NATIONAL SECURITY ADVISER TO TRY TO UNDERSTAND WHAT IT IS THIS FOREIGN GOVERNMENT IS TRYING TO DO TO MANIPULATE THEIR POSITION AGAINST THE U.S.

Michael Flynn pleaded guilty to lying to the FBI concerning his discussions with the Russian ambassador in the days and weeks before the end of the Obama administration. He eventually withdrew his plea after replacing his legal team with attorney Sidney Powell. After William Barr became attorney general, it was revealed that FBI and Justice Department personnel may have acted improperly in not only the Flynn case, but in the entire Russia investigation that targeted the Trump administration.

Judge Sullivan, the trial judge in the Flynn case, was prepared to proceed with the Flynn trial until Barr and the Justice Department told Sullivan they wanted to abandon the prosecution of Flynn even after his admission of guilt.

13.
Ghostwriters in the Sky

I MET MY FRIEND FOR LUNCH AGAIN on October 12, 2017. It was a sunny day, but getting cold so we decided to skip the ocean view from the covered but breezy deck and eat inside. When I set my purse down on the seat between us in our booth, she looked down and saw that I'd brought my copy of Hillary's *What Happened*. It was sort of sticking out of my purse.

"That's her new book, isn't it?" she asked.

"Yes it is. Do you want to see it?" I removed the book from my purse and slid it toward her just as our waiter appeared, menus in hand. He glanced down at the book and gave me a momentary one-eyed stare but said only that he would be back shortly to take our order.

My friend tapped with her index finger on Hillary's name printed on the cover and asked, "Did she really write this herself?"

"Well," I said, "Hillary Clinton is the author of record, but she freely admits that she had a team of three others helping her—she names them and gives a short bio for each in the 'acknowledgements' section of the book."

"It's pretty thick," said my friend as she opened it to a random page near the back, "—more than 500 pages. That would be pretty hard for one person to write in just a few months without any help."

"You're right about that." I said. "Years ago you would never know if a politician or celebrity wrote a single word of what was in print. The ghostwriter's identity was never disclosed, but these days it's completely different. You don't even hear the word 'ghostwriter' anymore. Now it's a 'team effort' or the celebrity author has a 'writing partner.' Sometimes that person's name will even appear on the cover below the celebrity author's name—usually in tiny 'mice-type'."

At this point, it was clear that I'd given my friend way more information than she cared to hear, so I turned the conversation toward some topics of mutual personal interest.

WE STEPPED OUTSIDE TO THE DECK after lunch and found some open seating on a bench near the railing. It was my friend who brought up the subject of Hillary's memoir once again.

"I've heard she's sold a lot of books."

"Yes," I said. "I read somewhere that it sold 300,000 copies in just the first week. We can see some of the reviews, if you're interested." Without waiting for an answer, I opened the Safari web browser on my iPhone to the book description page for *What Happened* at one of the largest online retail outlets.

The review section of the page on that date showed that *What Happened* had received 1,945 customer reviews with an average rating of 4.8 out a possible five stars. Eighty-six percent of the reviewers had given the book a 5-star rating with just 7% giving it one star.

When I got home that day, I searched around the internet for any updated sales figures or other commentary on Hillary's memoir. What I found most interesting was a September 14, 2017, article at ZeroHedge.com by Tyler Durden that showed how hundreds of one-star reviews were removed from the retailer's book page on September 12. A screen shot from 2:55 PM shows that there were 1,616 reviews with an average rating of 3.3 out of 5-stars. Three hours later the same page shows only 442 reviews with an average 4.9 stars rating. Speaking to *Fortune*, a spokesperson for the retailer said:

IN THE CASE OF A MEMOIR, THE SUBJECT OF THE BOOK IS THE AUTHOR AND THEIR VIEWS. IT'S NOT OUR ROLE TO DECIDE WHAT A CUSTOMER WOULD VIEW AS HELPFUL OR UNHELPFUL IN MAKING THEIR DECISION. WE DO HOWEVER HAVE MECHANISMS IN PLACE TO ENSURE THAT THE VOICES OF MANY DO NOT DROWN OUT THE VOICES OF A FEW AND WE REMOVE CUSTOMER REVIEWS THAT VIOLATE OUR COMMUNITY GUIDELINES.

Visitors to a book's product page are able to rate individual reviews as "helpful" or "not helpful" by clicking the "yes" or "no" button in answer to the question, "Was this review helpful to you?" When I went back to the product page for Hillary's memoir, the displayed "critical" review that visitors to the page found most helpful was a 2-star review that had been posted on September

14, 2017. A total of 16,786 people found this particular review helpful. It read as follows:

"REVIEW DELETED—AGAIN"

I WROTE A VERIFIED PURCHASE REVIEW AND IT HAS BEEN DELETED 3 TIMES. IF . . . DOESN'T LIKE WHAT WE HAVE TO SAY, DON'T ASK FOR INPUT.

I RECENTLY READ A DECIDEDLY sarcastic blog post that asked the question, "How will the poor Clinton family possibly survive now that neither holds public office?" The writer went on to make the point that because neither Bill, nor especially Hillary, was in a position to deliver "favors" to special donors and contributors, that their future income might suffer a precipitous drop.

I didn't have to ponder the question for very long before I told myself, "At least they won't have to worry about money in 2017, thanks to Hillary's latest book." Although the size of Mrs Clinton's advance from publisher Simon & Schuster has not been reported—or leaked—as yet, people who know about book sales and marketing have suggested that she is likely to earn at least $20 million from *What Happened*. By comparison, Bill Clinton's 2004 autobiography, *My Life*, has earned him an estimated $30 million, and Hillary reportedly received an advance of $14 million for *Hard Choices*, a memoir of her years as secretary of state, published in 2014. Mrs Clinton is earning extra money at her sold-out book tour events. Prices started at $45 for a seat at the Auditorium Theater in Chicago on October 30, 2017, while a $2,375 VIP Platinum Ticket for the October 23rd Montreal event would bestow (after purchase) upon those most loyal of Hillary supporters front-row seating for two, a backstage meet-and-greet including a photo with Mrs Clinton plus a signed copy of *What Happened*.

For Bill Clinton, the good news is that even before the forthcoming release of his first novel, a collaborative effort with prolific author James Patterson, it was announced that Showtime premium cable network will develop a drama series based on their book, *The President is Missing*.

A significant income source for the Clintons in the past has been their ability to land lucrative speaking gigs from Wall Street bankers and international business consortia, but since the election—not so much. Hillary has spoken at more than twenty events since the presidential election and up until June 2017—but nothing like the Goldman Sachs and Morgan Stanley speeches of past years. Instead, Hillary gave a speech in Scranton, Pennsylvania to the Society of Irish Women St. Patrick's Day Dinner (March 17), the Planned Parenthood Gala: Celebrating 100 Years Strong (May 2), a commencement address at Wellesley College (May 26) and other like events.

As might be expected, Clinton Foundation donations are down from the levels of 2016 and prior years, and an important outreach of the foundation, the Clinton Global Initiative, ceased operations after twelve years. The staff of 22 personnel was terminated effective April 15, 2017. However, subsequent rumors that the entire Clinton Foundation was being closed down were false.

But as the song sort-of goes, "Don't Cry for Me, Morgan Stanley." A 2016 *Forbes* estimate of the Clintons' net worth was reported to be $240 million.

14.
And the Winner Is . . .

THERE WERE JUST FOUR STATES IN the Clinton v. Trump presidential election where the margin of victory was less than 1%. Donald Trump won three of those states—Michigan, Pennsylvania and Wisconsin—with a combined total of 46 Electoral College votes. Hillary Clinton won the 4 Electoral College votes (ECV) from the state of New Hampshire. The vote margins compiled from data at ballotpedia.org are shown below:

- Michigan (16 ECV)
    Trump won by 10,704 votes
- Pennsylvania (20 ECV)
    Trump won by 44,292 votes
- Wisconsin (10 ECV)
    Trump won by 22,748 votes
- New Hampshire (4 ECV)
    Clinton won by 2,736 votes

From the total 538 Electoral College votes to be cast, 270 represents the minimum majority needed to win. In the event that no candidate reaches the 270 vote threshold, then the winner is determined by a vote of the state delegations in the House of Representatives, selecting from the three candidates with the highest electoral vote count. The House tally is determined with each state having just a single vote.

The razor-thin margins in four states suggest that a few thousand votes could have dramatically changed the outcome of the 2016 presidential election. When one considers that there were seven state electors who cast their vote for neither of the two front runners, it is not hard to imagine a situation where the final selection of our president might have been determined by the House of Representatives. Such a scenario visited upon us in 2016 would likely have created a huge political crisis as the House—the legislative body closest to the people—selected Donald J. Trump as president in the face of Hillary Clinton's popular vote plurality.

A detailed report in *The New York Times* online "The UpShot" section published shortly before the November 8 election contained the results of national and individual state pre-election polling. The report, which combined the results of ten nationally-recognized polls, also included a statistical estimate of the probability that the poll favorite would win.

The report showed Hillary Clinton the predicted winner of the popular vote by 45.9% to 42.8%, a 3.1% margin. Based on the results for individual states the report predicted that Clinton had overall an 84% probability of winning the election.

When the election results were tabulated we learned that Hillary Clinton won the popular vote by a 2.1% margin. Surprisingly, the UpShot report polling summary was remarkably close to the actual result, but for the individual states, not so much. The following were the predicted results from polling data for the seven states that Mrs Clinton was expected win by small margins:

- Florida for Clinton by 2.2% margin and 67% probability of winning the state.

- Michigan for Clinton by 2.4% margin and 93% probability of winning the state.

- Nevada for Clinton by 2.1% margin and 68% probability of winning the state.

- New Hampshire for Clinton by 3.1% margin and 89% probability of winning the state.

- North Carolina for Clinton by 2.3% margin and 64% probability of winning the state.

- Pennsylvania for Clinton by 4.1% margin and 89% probability of winning the state.

- Wisconsin for Clinton by 4.1% margin and 93% probability of winning the state.

When the final votes were tallied, we learned that Donald Trump had won five of the seven close races that the UpShot prediction had given to Hillary Clinton. Among the seven states, Mrs Clinton won 10 electoral votes; Mr Trump won 90.

I WATCHED THE ELECTION RESULTS with a close friend on election night. He had been an early Bernie Sanders supporter but cast his vote for Donald Trump earlier in the day. Although hopeful for a Trump victory, I honestly had little confidence that he could win.

As the polls closed in the East at 8PM, Clinton was declared the winner in Maryland, New Jersey and Massachusetts, adding to the four states and the District of

Columbia that she was awarded earlier in the evening. Those wins would place her at 68 electoral votes while Donald Trump had 76 after he was declared the winner in Oklahoma.

One hour later, with Donald Trump ahead in five key "battleground" states, including Florida, international stock markets and U.S. equity futures had already begun to sell off. The Mexican peso was headed toward its biggest one-day fall since 2011, and the 10-year U.S. Treasury bond yield had dropped from 1.85% to 1.75%.

Now it was getting exciting. My friend said I had a "surprised" expression on my face. I don't doubt it. At 9:20 PM Trump was leading 130 electoral votes to 97, and he was being given better than 50-50 odds to win the election. At a Trump party in Manhattan the crowds watched the Fox News channel on giant screens and cheered wildly as one state after another was declared for their candidate.

Some of the details that follow were extracted from a *New York Times* running interactive commentary among multiple *Times* reporters during live election night coverage and published at nytimes.com.

At 10:00PM the mood at Hillary's Election Central improved slightly as Virginia was declared in her favor, but soon some media reporters were suggesting that Republicans might make a full sweep of the election: presidency, Senate and House of Representatives.

By 10:45PM *The New York Times* called Ohio for Donald Trump. Ohio had always been considered a bellwether state: in recent elections, no candidate has won the presidency without winning in Ohio. Dow Jones Industrials futures were now down by 600 points.

By 10:56PM North Carolina and Florida had been called for Trump. Four minutes later, the polls closed in the West and Clinton was declared the winner in California and Hawaii. By 11:25PM the *Times* reporters acknowledged that Clinton would need to prevail in all three states—Wisconsin, Michigan and Pennsylvania—in order to have any chance at winning, and yet the returns showed that she was behind except in Pennsylvania where she maintained a small but steadily diminishing lead. Five minutes later Fox News called Wisconsin for Trump.

By 12:20AM Dow futures were down by 800 points. As scenes on television switched between the ebullient crowds at Trump Headquarters and the sullen faces at Clinton events, few American observers were unsure of the ultimate outcome. The AP called Pennsylvania for Trump at 1:39AM.

John Podesta, Hillary's campaign manager, arrived at the Javits Center about 2:00AM, telling supporters to go home and get some sleep. He adds:

> WE'LL HAVE MORE TO SAY TOMORROW. YOUR VOICES AND YOUR ENTHUSIASM MEAN SO MUCH TO HER AND TO TIM AND TO ALL OF US. WE ARE SO PROUD OF YOU, AND WE ARE SO PROUD OF HER. SHE HAS DONE AN AMAZING JOB, AND SHE IS NOT DONE YET. LET'S GET THOSE VOTES COUNTED, AND LET'S GET THIS DONE.

Ten minutes later, the Associated Press projected that Donald Trump had won the election to become the next president of the United States. At 2:48AM Mike Pence introduced President-elect Trump to the crowd at the Hilton Hotel. Donald Trump said:

> I'VE JUST RECEIVED A CALL FROM SECRETARY CLINTON.
>
> SHE CONGRATULATED US — IT'S ABOUT US — ON OUR VICTORY, AND I

CONGRATULATED HER AND HER FAMILY ON A VERY, VERY HARD-FOUGHT CAMPAIGN. I MEAN, SHE — SHE FOUGHT VERY HARD.

HILLARY HAS WORKED VERY LONG AND VERY HARD OVER A LONG PERIOD OF TIME, AND WE OWE HER A MAJOR DEBT OF GRATITUDE FOR HER SERVICE TO OUR COUNTRY.

I MEAN THAT VERY SINCERELY.

NOW IT'S TIME FOR AMERICA TO BIND THE WOUNDS OF DIVISION; HAVE TO GET TOGETHER. TO ALL REPUBLICANS AND DEMOCRATS AND INDEPENDENTS ACROSS THIS NATION, I SAY IT IS TIME FOR US TO COME TOGETHER AS ONE UNITED PEOPLE.

IT'S TIME. I PLEDGE TO EVERY CITIZEN OF OUR LAND THAT I WILL BE PRESIDENT FOR ALL AMERICANS, AND THIS IS SO IMPORTANT TO ME.

Donald Trump's victory speech continued for several minutes. My friend let himself out and went home. I fell asleep on the sofa—smiling.

And what had become of the financial markets that had cratered in the early morning hours as some nervous investors realized that Donald Trump could be the next president of the United States? By the time that stocks opened in the U.S. on Wednesday morning, nearly all the futures losses had been erased. By the end of the day stocks were up slightly from their previous close. In the ensuing months and up until the economic downturn associated with the COVID-19 pandemic, financial markets continued to make gains with hardly a look back.

GREEN PARTY CANDIDATE JILL STEIN announced shortly after the election that she intended to request recounts in Pennsylvania, Michigan and Wisconsin according to a November 24, 2016, article in the *Chicago Tribune*. "This has been a hack-riddled election," she said. "We have voting machines that are extremely hack-friendly in an election that's been very contentious."

Stein raised $4.5 million to fund the recount effort that was eventually joined by the Clinton campaign. What wasn't clear was why such an effort would be promoted by the Green Party candidate who overall received less than one percent of the popular vote. Donald Trump and others charged that it was just a scam to raise money, a charge that Stein vehemently denied.

A 10-day recount was actually completed in Wisconsin with the result that Donald Trump actually gained an additional 131 votes. A recount effort in Michigan was never completed after being halted by the Michigan Supreme Court. A federal judge in Pennsylvania stopped the recount there before it began.

ON MAY 11, 2017, PRESIDENT DONALD Trump signed an executive order creating a commission aimed at investigating alleged vote fraud in America's election system. Vice President Mike Pence was the designated chairman of the group named the "Presidential Commission on Election Integrity."

The commission's second meeting took place on September 12, 2017, in Manchester, New Hampshire. Earlier, commission co-chairman and Kansas Secretary of State Kris Kobach charged in a column at Breitbart.com that fraud committed by Democratic voters changed the New Hampshire election results in 2016. The charge was based on a report issued by New Hampshire Secretary of State Bill Gardner.

Hillary Clinton beat Donald Trump in New Hampshire by less than 2,800 votes in the November 2016 election, and Maggie Hassan, the Democratic challenger to incumbent Republican Kelly Ayotte, won by just over 1,000 votes. New Hampshire's four electoral votes were awarded to Hillary Clinton.

Gardner's report blamed New Hampshire's same-day voter registration law. While new resident drivers have 60 days to secure a New Hampshire driver's license, some 5,300 voters who registered with out-of-state driver's licenses on Election Day were found to have never subsequently applied for the New Hampshire license nor registered a vehicle in the state.

A fraud would be committed if a resident of a nearby state such as Vermont, Maine, Massachusetts or New York traveled to New Hampshire on Election Day or earlier, registered to vote and cast their ballot. The fraudulent voter would have likely cast a vote in his or her home state as well.

We do not know, of course, to which candidate each of the 5,300 cast their vote or even if extenuating circumstances could account for why the votes were legal and not fraudulent, but any large number of votes that could be considered fraudulent could have easily upset the results of the close Senate and presidential races in New Hampshire in 2016.

As might be expected, the very establishment of President Trump's commission and the report of suspected voter fraud in New Hampshire has caused a storm of outrage from the Left. In a September 13, 2017, *Washington Times* Op-Ed, talk show host and author Tammi Bruce responds:

> DURING LAST YEAR'S ELECTION, THE PRESIDENT VOICED WHAT WE KNOW — THAT VOTER FRAUD EXISTS. THE ONLY QUESTION IS TO WHAT DEGREE, AND THAT'S THE MISSION OF THE COMMISSION.
>
> FOR ANYONE WHO DISMISSES CONCERNS ABOUT VOTER FRAUD, THE UNHINGED REACTION BY THE LEFT AT INVESTIGATING IT SHOULD, AT THE VERY LEAST, MAKE A LOGICAL PERSON WONDER WHAT THEY'RE SO CONCERNED ABOUT.
>
> AFTER ALL, IF YOU BELIEVE THE ISSUE IS FALSE, OR AT THE MOST AN IRRELEVANT FACTOR IN END RESULTS, YOU SHOULD WELCOME CONFIRMATION OF THAT FACT. UNLESS, OF COURSE, ONE FEARS THE

ACTUAL OUTCOME MAY PROVE HOW VOTER FRAUD IMPACTS LOCAL AND STATE RACES TO THE POINT OF SHIFTING THE BALANCE OF POWER IN WASHINGTON, D.C.

15.
What Really Happened

ANALYSTS HAVE COME UP WITH multiple reasons why Hillary Clinton was unable to prevail in the 2016 presidential election—a few, even, have been documented in her memoir, *What Happened*. While I don't pretend to have any special insight or even anything particularly original to add, I believe it is worthwhile to explore theories that have been advanced by analysts and pundits from both sides of the political spectrum.

The FBI investigation of Hillary Clinton's private email server—especially James Comey's late October 2016 decision to send a letter to lawmakers informing them of his agency's renewed probe—ranks high on

Hillary's list of reasons why she lost the election. But if we look at the chain of events leading to Comey's decision, we learn that (1) the probe was reopened because new clintonmail.com emails and potentially-sensitive state department documents were found on Anthony Weiner's laptop, (2) the emails and documents were on the laptop because Mrs Clinton's deputy chief of staff, Huma Abedin, routinely printed documents and communicated by email with Mrs Clinton and other members of the state department staff when working from home using her husband's laptop.

Now, it seems reasonable to assume that if (3) Mrs Clinton had not made the decision to install and use an email server in her Chappaqua home—and later at Platte River Networks—and (4) she had not chosen to use a private email account in an effort to shield her communications from potential FOIA disclosure and (5) Mrs Clinton and her top aides had not been "extremely careless" in the handling of classified information, then there would have been no late October bombshell letter sent to lawmakers from then-Director Comey.

It is acknowledged that Mrs Clinton admits some responsibility for the email imbroglio, calling her decision to use a private email server while secretary of state a "boneheaded mistake." But it was more than that; the email scandal hurt her because there was no escaping the fact that she was personally responsible for it, and because the evasive responses and manufactured excuses that she put forth during interviews further reinforced the opinion held by many voters that she was dishonest and corrupt.

In a Daily Beast column published six days after the election, author Jonathan Alter argues that the election wasn't won by Donald Trump as much as it was lost by Hillary Clinton. Alter writes:

> ABOUT 6 MILLION FEWER VOTERS TURNED OUT THIS YEAR THAN IN 2012, WITH AROUND TWO-THIRDS OF THE NO-SHOWS BEING DEMOCRATS. MILLIONS OF OTHER DEMOCRATS VOTED ONLY IN DOWN-BALLOT RACES. IN MICHIGAN, WHERE CLINTON LOST BY AROUND 13,000 VOTES, SOME ANALYSTS ESTIMATE THAT 90,000 DEMOCRATS LEFT THE TOP LINE BLANK.

Others have argued that Mrs Clinton failed to deliver what many voters wanted most: change. Instead, she represented the worst of the corporate-financed Washington Beltway establishment. It didn't help that much of Hillary's pitch was weak on issues and was instead devoted to calling out Donald Trump's obvious—according to her—character flaws and what a dangerous and unreliable president he would make.

In a December 26, 2016, salon.com article "Why Donald Trump won — and how Hillary Clinton lost: 13 Theories Explain the Stunning Election," originally appearing at alternet.org, the authors wrote:

CLINTON ALSO LACKED A STRONG CENTRAL MESSAGE. HER GENERAL ELECTION CAMPAIGN FOCUSED ALMOST EXCLUSIVELY ON TRUMP'S UNFITNESS FOR OFFICE. SHE HAD EXTENSIVE PROPOSALS ON HER WEBSITE, BUT THEY SEEMED MORE LIKE WONKY, UNINSPIRING TWEAKS TO OBAMACARE, MINIMUM WAGE AND PAID FAMILY LEAVE, NOT A GRAND VISION. EVEN THOSE WHO WERE FOR HER WERE HARD-PRESSED TO SAY WHAT EXACTLY SHE STOOD FOR AND WHAT SHE PLANNED TO DO, OR WHAT HER LEGACY MIGHT BE.

Some have questioned why with only days remaining before the election, Hillary's campaign held a rally featuring the candidate in Arizona—a state that she didn't need to win—and failed to have her make a single campaign stop in Wisconsin—where not winning definitely contributed to her loss. A cynic might suggest that the decision by Hillary Clinton to skip Wisconsin made no practical difference as she lost both Wisconsin (zero campaign trips) and Pennsylvania (ten campaign trips) by the same 0.7% margin.

Michael Moore, American film maker, author and liberal political activist, weighed in early with a prediction for the presidential election. In July 2016 Moore wrote an essay, "5 Reasons Why Trump Will Win," posted at michaelmoore.com. While denigrating then-candidate Trump, Moore cautioned that Democrats were "living in denial." He wrote:

AND IF YOU BELIEVE HILLARY CLINTON IS GOING TO BEAT TRUMP WITH FACTS AND SMARTS AND LOGIC, THEN YOU OBVIOUSLY MISSED THE PAST YEAR OF 56 PRIMARIES AND CAUCUSES WHERE 16 REPUBLICAN CANDIDATES TRIED THAT AND EVERY KITCHEN SINK THEY COULD THROW AT TRUMP AND NOTHING COULD STOP HIS JUGGERNAUT.

Summarizing Moore's 5 Reasons, he offers the following:

1. Moore believed that Trump would focus much of his attention on the four formerly blue states in the rust belt of the upper Great Lakes– Michigan, Ohio, Pennsylvania and Wisconsin. Trump has promised to turn around the economic decline in the region by rolling back NAFTA and canceling TPP, trade deals that had long been supported by the Clintons. In Michigan, Trump was widely applauded when he threatened the imposition of a high tariff on Ford autos imported from Mexico if the company followed through with plans to close a Michigan plant and move production south of the border.

2. Moore said that Trump had energized the "Angry White Man" who looks about and can't help but see that his power, influence and values have been steadily diminished under years of liberal governance, and he believes that a Trump presidency is the only thing that will stop and reverse it.

3. Moore said that Hillary was a hugely unpopular candidate. Nearly 70% of all voters think she is untrustworthy and dishonest. Moore writes, "No Democrat, and certainly no independent, is waking up on November 8th excited to run out and vote for Hillary the way they did the day Obama became president or when Bernie was on the primary ballot."

4. Sanders supporters were dispirited. Moore believed that while most would still vote for Hillary, some would switch to a third-party candidate or simply stay home. It's unlikely that any of them would expend much effort promoting Hillary's candidacy. She might have raised their enthusiasm some if she had picked a different running mate, especially if she had chosen another woman. Presumably, Moore meant that Elizabeth Warren would have been a better choice for vice president than Tim Kaine.

5. Jesse Ventura was a professional wrestler who successfully ran for Governor of Minnesota, serving from

1999 to 2003. In what Moore calls the "Jesse Ventura Effect," he sees many voters supporting Donald Trump as a political statement—a poke in the eye by angry voters upset over the broken political system.

I give Michael Moore full credit on Reason #1 and #3 and partial credit on #4. That's 2-1/2 points out of a possible 5, but no one can deny that he was spot on with the bottom line of his prediction. Michael Moore is a smart guy; too bad he hates the president.

Beyond the presidential election, it is a fact that Democrats nationwide have sustained significant losses at the ballot box in recent years. During President Obama's two terms, Democrats lost 9 U.S. Senate seats, 62 House seats, 12 governorships and more than 950 seats among state legislatures.

The reason for these losses is not complicated. Since before the Obama presidency the Democratic Party has moved decidedly further left. Remember Barack Obama's speech at the University of Missouri days before the 2008 presidential election? He proudly called out to his minions, "We are five days away from fundamentally transforming the United States of America."

Despite the election losses, Democrats appear to have doubled-down on the notion of transformation by advancing well-left-of-center politicians like Elizabeth Warren, Kamala Harris and Democratic National Committee Chairman Thomas Perez.

Perhaps Democrats are playing the "long game." The party appears to have made a conscious decision to sacrifice the support of union members and blue collar workers in favor of the potentially much larger and faster growing voting blocks of minorities and immigrants. Exit polls from the 2016 election reveal the following generalized results:

- Trump voters included whites, Christians, individuals over 40 years old, individuals with family incomes over $50,000, Midwesterners, Southerners, and suburban and rural area residents.

- Clinton voters included minorities, Jews and other non-Christians, individuals under 40 years old, individuals with family incomes less than $50,000, residents from the Northeast and West, and city-dwellers.

If the 2016 presidential election returns from the rust belt states mean anything, the Democratic Party may have been premature in its decision to pursue a platform based upon identify politics, but someday they may be rewarded for that decision. A Pew Research Center report published on April 25, 2016, stated that Millennials—those born between 1981 and 1999—have surpassed the number of Baby Boomers, those born between 1946 and 1964. The report attributes the increase in the number of Millennials to immigration:

THE MILLENNIAL GENERATION CONTINUES TO GROW AS YOUNG IMMIGRANTS EXPAND ITS RANKS. BOOMERS – WHOSE GENERATION WAS DEFINED BY THE BOOM IN U.S. BIRTHS FOLLOWING WORLD WAR II – ARE OLDER AND THEIR NUMBERS SHRINKING AS THE NUMBER OF DEATHS AMONG THEM EXCEEDS THE NUMBER OF OLDER IMMIGRANTS ARRIVING IN THE COUNTRY.

The Republicans Party will ignore these data and the warning signs at their own peril.

DONALD TRUMP TAPPED INTO THE emotions of middle-class workers who felt that the American dream had passed beyond their reach. The "forgotten men and women" had no one in Washington to hear their voices, but Donald Trump promised to listen, and he promised that they would be forgotten no longer. Many believe that it was the forgotten men and women who decided the election. Chris Matthews, political commentator and host on MSNBC, said in September 2016:

> A LOT OF THIS SUPPORT FOR TRUMP, WITH ALL HIS FLAWS WHICH HE DISPLAYS REGULARLY, IS ABOUT THE COUNTRY — PATRIOTIC FEELINGS PEOPLE HAVE, THEY FEEL LIKE THE COUNTRY HAS BEEN LET DOWN. OUR ELITE LEADERS ON ISSUES LIKE IMMIGRATION, THEY DON'T REGULATE ANY IMMIGRATION IT SEEMS. THEY DON'T REGULATE TRADE TO OUR ADVANTAGE, TO THE WORKING MAN OR WORKING WOMAN'S ADVANTAGE. THEY TAKE US INTO STUPID WARS. THEIR KIDS DON'T FIGHT BUT OUR KIDS DO.

At a "Thank You Tour 2016" rally in West Allis, Wisconsin, on December 13, 2016, President-elect Trump held his supporters in rapt attention as he related his thoughts and emotions as the election returns came in that fateful evening:

SO IT BEGAN WITH PHONY EXIT POLLS. AND I GOT A CALL FROM MY DAUGHTER AT ABOUT 5 O'CLOCK, AND SHE WAS CALLED BY PEOPLE IN THEIR BUSINESS. AND HER HUSBAND, JARED, GREAT GUY, HE WAS CALLED. THEN THEY CALLED ME AND THEY SAID: 'I'M SORRY, DAD. IT LOOKS REALLY BAD. LOOKS REALLY, REALLY BAD.'

SO I SORT OF THOUGHT I LOST, AND I WAS OK WITH THAT. I WOULDN'T SAY GREAT. IN FACT, I CALLED MY VICE PRESIDENT AND I SAID, 'IT'S NOT LOOKING GOOD.' RIGHT, MIKE? I SAID NOT LOOKING GOOD.

The president-elect reminded the crowd of the pace of the campaign in the days just before the election and a conversation with wife Melania. He then continued:

THEY KNEW THEY WERE GONNA WIN UNTIL THE FINAL WEEK. THEY KNEW BAD THINGS WERE HAPPENING, AND I GOT A GOOD SIGN WHEN FOUR DAYS BEFORE THE END — I CALLED UP MIKE — THEY JUST CANCELED THE FIREWORKS. IT WAS

A FRONT-PAGE STORY. THEY CANCELED. NOW USUALLY YOU CANCEL FIREWORKS BECAUSE YOU DON'T WANT FIREWORKS IF YOU'RE GONNA LOSE, RIGHT? . . .

THEN IT HAPPENED, FOLKS, OUT OF NOWHERE. BOY, THAT MAP WAS GETTING RED AS HELL. THAT MAP — THAT MAP WAS BLEEDING RED. . . .

I'LL NEVER FORGET WHEN THEY WERE ON THE MAP AND THEY PUT UP WISCONSIN, AND HE SAID, 'THERE IS NO PATH FOR HILLARY CLINTON TO BECOME PRESIDENT. DONALD TRUMP IS YOUR NEXT PRESIDENT OF THE UNITED STATES.' BECAUSE OF YOU. SO I WANNA THANK — I WANNA THANK THE PEOPLE OF WISCONSIN. YOU'RE INCREDIBLE PEOPLE.

The audience could not have been more excited as they cheered their hero.

16.
Could Bernie Have Won?

IT WASN'T LONG AFTER THE ELECTION results were known that we began to hear complaints from Sanders supporters and others that he could have beaten Donald Trump had Bernie been the Democratic Party's candidate.

One of the "others" who weighed in somewhat later on the subject was political opinion writer Brent Budowsky. I put him in the "other" category because of the revelation in one of the leaked WikiLeaks emails from Budowsky to Clinton campaign manager John Podesta. In that July 1, 2015, email the writer warns against the Clinton campaign running negative ads against Sanders because those Sanders supporters would be needed in Hillary's battle against her yet-to-be-named

Republican opponent. Budowsky outlined a plan to Podesta stating that he would continue writing highly supportive and complementary articles about Sanders so that when the votes of Sanders' supporters were needed, he (Budowsky) would be a trusted agent whose reasoned advice to support Hillary could be confidently followed.

It is stunning to consider that this apparent subterfuge was going on a year before the Democratic National Convention and Hillary's nomination. A LifeZette.com column by Kathryn Blackhurst that was my source for the above material was aptly titled, "WikiLeaks: Liberal Columnist Tried to 'Trojan Horse' Bernie" and the subtitle, "Podesta emails show writer gave Sanders good ink to ultimately push his backers to Clinton." Nevertheless, Budowsky put forward some interesting ideas on why Bernie might have won. In a May 15, 2017, column at The Hill, he wrote in part:

> SANDERS WOULD HAVE WON IN 2016 BECAUSE HE ALONE CALLED FOR A PRESIDENT TO LEAD THE CHARGE FOR GIVING EVERY AMERICAN AN OPPORTUNITY FOR A COLLEGE EDUCATION, OFFERING TUITION-FREE PUBLIC COLLEGE ENROLLMENT.

SANDERS WOULD HAVE WON IN 2016 BECAUSE HE ALONE CALLED FOR THE BOLD, TRANSFORMING AND EGALITARIAN ECONOMIC POLICIES THAT ARE THE ANTITHESIS OF TRUMP'S CRONY CAPITALISM, WHICH HE WOULD HAVE EXPOSED IN WAYS CLINTON COULD NOT.

SANDERS WOULD HAVE WON IN 2016 BECAUSE HE OFFERED THE HONEST AND TRUE CHOICE FOR CHANGE AND, AS A POLITICAL LEADER FAR MORE LIKED AND TRUSTED THAN TRUMP COULD EVER DREAM OF BEING, WAS THE ULTIMATE MESSENGER FOR THE GREAT CAUSE A MAJORITY OF VOTERS WERE WILLING TO SUPPORT.

SANDERS WOULD HAVE WON IN 2016 BECAUSE HE DID NOT NEED AN ARMY OF CONSULTANTS TO TELL HIM WHAT HE BELIEVES AND SELL IT LIKE SOAP SUDS, AND VOTERS SENSED THAT SANDERS WAS SPEAKING FROM POWERFUL AND STRONGLY-HELD CONVICTIONS THAT HE WOULD IMPLEMENT AS PRESIDENT ON THEIR BEHALF.

FBI DIRECTOR JAMES COMEY WOULD NEVER HAVE INFLUENCED THE ELECTION BECAUSE SANDERS NEVER USED PRIVATE EMAILS THAT NEEDED TO BE

INVESTIGATED IN THE FIRST PLACE. VLADIMIR PUTIN WOULD NEVER HAVE BEEN ABLE TO SUCCESSFULLY HACK OUR DEMOCRACY BECAUSE, IF HE HAD STOLEN EVERY SECRET ABOUT BERNIE SANDERS, VOTERS WOULD HAVE RALLIED BEHIND HIM EVEN MORE!

While I can't agree with much contained in Mr Budowsky's emotional arguments, they do provide some insight into what lurks behind much liberal political thought.

Moving on to some partially-reasoned commentary, *Washington Post* writer Philip Bump opens his November 13, 2016, column, "Of Course Bernie Sanders Could Have Beaten Donald Trump" with a stated opinion by the candidate himself:

ASKED BY *THE POST* IF HE THOUGHT HE COULD HAVE BEATEN DONALD TRUMP, BERNIE SANDERS WAS TEMPERATE IN HIS REPLY.

"I HESITATE TO BE A MONDAY MORNING QUARTERBACK," HE SAID. "IN MY HEART OF HEARTS, I THINK THERE'S A GOOD CHANCE I COULD HAVE DEFEATED TRUMP, BUT WHO KNOWS."

Mr Bump uses somewhat circular reasoning in providing an answer to the question, "Could Bernie Sanders have beaten Donald Trump?" He states correctly that the election was very close—that 109,000 votes in Michigan, Wisconsin and Pennsylvania made the difference, and that numerous other scenarios involving a relatively small number of votes could have resulted in a Clinton victory. Then, since we can agree that Hillary came *close* to winning, then we can agree that she *could* have won. And if she could have won, then it follows that Bernie could have won as well. *Huh? Where is Scooby when you need him?*

Mr Bump presents some decidedly more reasoned thoughts in response to the more difficult question he poses, "Did Sanders stand a better chance of beating Trump?" He mentions a privately-commissioned Gravis Marketing poll in which Sanders bested Donald Trump, but we understand that such polls can be biased.

A more reasoned explanation from the author as to why Sanders might have done better than Mrs Clinton in the race against Donald Trump is that Bernie actually beat Hillary in the Michigan and Wisconsin primary elections. That Bernie had strength in the Midwest from his trade policy, but with the added concern that it might be offset by questionable support for his socialist solutions, was well-explained in the following paragraph by Mr Bump:

IT'S SORT OF TAKEN AS AN ARTICLE OF FAITH THAT SANDERS WOULD HAVE EASILY FLIPPED THOSE RUST BELT STATES THAT CLINTON LOST. IT'S CLEAR THAT HIS VEHEMENCE ON TRADE WAS MORE IN LINE WITH WHAT MANY VOTERS IN THAT REGION WERE HOPING TO HEAR. WAS THAT ENOUGH? HOW WOULD SANDERS HAVE FARED IN THE FACE OF ATTACKS ON HIS POLITICAL PHILOSOPHY? SOCIALISM IS BROADLY VIEWED POSITIVELY BY DEMOCRATS ACCORDING TO GALLUP, BUT IS WIDELY UNPOPULAR AMONG REPUBLICANS. IT'S MOSTLY YOUNGER PEOPLE WHO VIEW THE IDEA POSITIVELY, A GROUP THAT TENDS TO TURN OUT LESS REGULARLY THAN OTHERS. MORE WOULD HAVE DONE SO FOR SANDERS, CERTAINLY -- BUT WOULD THE GROUP OF DEMOCRATS THAT STAYED HOME SIMPLY HAVE MOVED FROM ONE DEMOGRAPHIC TO ANOTHER?

Mr Bump offers the following concluding remarks in response to the question of whether or not Bernie Sanders had a better chance of beating Donald Trump than did Hillary Clinton:

BUT IT'S IMPOSSIBLE TO KNOW IF HE WOULD HAVE HAD A BETTER CHANCE THAN DID CLINTON, IN PART BECAUSE HER CHANCE WAS VERY GOOD.

JUST, AS IT TURNED OUT, NOT GOOD ENOUGH.

Mr Bump can take some pride in the fact that Sanders' supporters followed closely what he wrote about their favorite politician. When Mr Bump stated incidentally in an April 18, 2016, column that he had calculated the average contribution to Bernie's campaign as closer to $29—slightly more than the $27 advertised by the candidate's campaign—he received a firestorm of complaints on social media.

While the content of the column was fairly neutral, the title read, "BERNIE SANDERS KEEPS SAYING HIS AVERAGE DONATION IS $27, BUT HIS OWN NUMBERS CONTRADICT THAT." It is not clear why the editor at the *Washington Post* responsible for that column's title failed to understand that Bernie's supporters would find the criticism implicit in the title to be petty and insulting. Mr Bump wrote a follow-up column the next day describing his experience with angry Sanders supporters.

While most of the writers that I read who dared explore the question of Bernie's electability in a match-up against Donald Trump avoided making an absolute yes-or-no declaration, there was one who expressed his certain belief that Sanders would have been the victor. The author is the two-time Pulitzer Prize-winning editorial cartoonist and columnist, David Horsey. His *Los Angeles Times* article, "President Sanders? Bernie Would Have Beaten Trump," was published on December 22, 2017. He wrote:

. . . . THIS TIME AROUND, MOST WORKING-CLASS WHITE VOTERS — MANY OF WHOM VOTED FOR BARACK OBAMA IN THE LAST TWO ELECTIONS — SAW CLINTON AS THE INCARNATION OF A POLITICAL ESTABLISHMENT THAT WAS INDIFFERENT TO THEIR STRUGGLES. THEY WERE WON OVER BY TRUMP'S BOASTS THAT HE WOULD PROTECT AMERICAN JOBS AND CHALLENGE THE INFLUENCE OF WALL STREET. WHO ELSE IN THE 2016 CAMPAIGN MADE SIMILAR PROMISES, WITH FAR MORE CONVICTION? BERNIE SANDERS, OF COURSE.

As to the contention that Bernie's socialist label disqualifies him in the minds of many conservatives and makes him a target for moderate and right-wing commentators, Horsey explains:

> SANDERS IS NOT A THREATENING, ALIEN FIGURE. HIS "SOCIALISM" WAS MOST PRONOUNCED IN HIS CALLS TO TAX THE WEALTHY AT A HIGHER RATE AND PROVIDE FREE COLLEGE TUITION AT STATE UNIVERSITIES — TWO IDEAS THAT ARE HARDLY RADICAL, GIVEN THAT BOTH WERE THE NORM IN THE AMERICA OF DWIGHT EISENHOWER AND JOHN F. KENNEDY.

In all honesty, David Horsey makes some surprisingly credible arguments.

17.
Russian Connections

IT SEEMED THAT FOR WEEKS BEFORE and months after the election we were bombarded with media reports and charges made by Democratic Party politicians of Trump campaign collusion with Russian hacking and general interference in the 2016 presidential race. The sheer and shrill volume of those reports increased dramatically beginning November 9, 2016, as the Hillary Campaign and the DNC cast about for some semi-plausible, Bart Simpson-approved excuse *(It wasn't me. I didn't do it!)* in order to account for their stunning election loss.

An Intelligence Community Assessment Report was published on January 6, 2017. Among the "Key Judgements" of the report was the following:

WE ASSESS RUSSIAN PRESIDENT VLADIMIR PUTIN ORDERED AN INFLUENCE CAMPAIGN IN 2016 AIMED AT THE US PRESIDENTIAL ELECTION. RUSSIA'S GOALS WERE TO UNDERMINE PUBLIC FAITH IN THE US DEMOCRATIC PROCESS, DENIGRATE SECRETARY CLINTON, AND HARM HER ELECTABILITY AND POTENTIAL PRESIDENCY. WE FURTHER ASSESS PUTIN AND THE RUSSIAN GOVERNMENT DEVELOPED A CLEAR PREFERENCE FOR PRESIDENT-ELECT TRUMP.

This important finding of the report is a conclusion apparently drawn from what only can be described as subjective evidence and innuendo that Russian government operatives hacked the DNC and provided the data to WikiLeaks. The arguments are not dissimilar to those put forth in the earlier "CrowdStrike" assessment commissioned by the DNC.

According to a Breitbart.com article from June 30, 2017, the first use of the "17 intelligence agencies" expression in the context of election interference by Russia is attributed to Hillary Clinton during the second Clinton-Trump debate. The expression was used many times in media reports throughout subsequent months. In a June 29, 2017, Associated Press article White House reporter Ken Thomas wrote:

ALL 17 US INTELLIGENCE AGENCIES HAVE AGREED RUSSIA WAS BEHIND LAST YEAR'S HACK OF DEMOCRATIC EMAIL SYSTEMS AND TRIED TO INFLUENCE THE 2016 ELECTION TO BENEFIT TRUMP.

The AP issued a retraction in early July shortly after an earlier *New York Times* retraction of a similarly erroneous report. Apparently it was three—not 17— intelligence agencies acting "under the aegis" of the Office of the Director of National Intelligence that agreed that Russian meddling had occurred. The three agencies, CIA, FBI and NSA, provided personnel working as a team to investigate and eventually generate the January 2017 Intelligence Community Assessment Report mentioned earlier in this chapter.

When I heard the first media reports of the findings of all "17 U.S intelligence agencies," my very first thought was, "Why do we need 17 separate U.S. intelligence agencies?" Maybe it's something Congress should be looking into.

BECAUSE THE ALLEGED DNC HACKING by the Russian Government took place in 2015 and 2016, it was expected that the Obama Administration would take steps to make sure it wouldn't continue. During a December 2016 press conference, the president disclosed that he had told President Vladimir Putin to "cut it out" when they met during the G-20 Summit in China in September. During his press conference the president said:

WHAT I WAS CONCERNED ABOUT IN PARTICULAR WAS MAKING SURE [THE HACK OF THE DEMOCRATIC NATIONAL CONVENTION] WASN'T COMPOUNDED BY POTENTIAL HACKING THAT COULD HAMPER VOTE COUNTING, AFFECT THE ACTUAL ELECTION PROCESS ITSELF.

The president added that our government had seen no further evidence of tampering of the election process after warning President Putin of serious consequences should the hacking continue. Nevertheless, on December 29, 2016, President Obama levied sanctions on the two Russian intelligence services believed to be involved in the hacking and expelled 35 officials working in the U.S. but suspected of being Russian intelligence agents.

THE MEDIA NARRATIVE OF TRUMP election campaign collusion with Russia continued prominently from November 9, 2016, until well after the May 2017 appointment of Robert Mueller as special counsel to investigate the matter. By early summer, Trump supporters were asking why the media wasn't reporting anything new about Russian meddling in the election. Was there nothing there? After all, leaking of information to the press on a variety of other subjects from unspecified government sources continued unabated.

It was especially curious why there had been no new evidence brought forward of collusion in the Russia matter after it was learned that Obama Administration officials apparently had open access to Trump team communications with foreign nationals. On January 12, 2017, a *Washington Post* article by David Ignatius disclosed that General Flynn and Russian Ambassador Kislyak had communicated by telephone on multiple occasions. The unmasking of Flynn's name by an Obama Administration official was a legal course of action if proper justification was filed beforehand, but leaking his name and substance of their conversations to the press was clearly illegal.

That the Obama Administration would refrain from leaking even the slightest hint of possible collusion discovered within the transcripts of communications between Russian officials and members of the Trump election campaign strains credulity. Maybe they could find nothing worth leaking.

It has been generally accepted as fact that neither Russia nor any other foreign entity attempted to change the vote count by hacking into U.S. voting machines. However, we know that countries sometimes try to influence the outcome of elections in other countries in other ways. A recent example was reported in a *Washington Times* article by Stephen Dinan on July 12, 2016. The author wrote:

THE STATE DEPARTMENT PAID HUNDREDS OF THOUSANDS OF DOLLARS IN TAXPAYERS GRANTS TO AN ISRAELI GROUP THAT USED THE MONEY TO BUILD A CAMPAIGN TO OUST PRIME MINISTER BENJAMIN NETAN-YAHU IN LAST YEAR'S ISRAELI PARLIA-MENTARY ELECTIONS, A CONGRESSIONAL INVESTIGATION CONCLUDED TUESDAY.

SOME $350,000 WAS SENT TO ONEVOICE, OSTENSIBLY TO SUPPORT THE GROUP'S EFFORTS TO BACK ISRAELI-

PALESTINIAN PEACE SETTLEMENT NEGOTIATIONS. BUT ONEVOICE USED THE MONEY TO BUILD A VOTER DATABASE, TRAIN ACTIVISTS AND HIRE A POLITICAL CONSULTING FIRM WITH TIES TO PRESIDENT OBAMA'S CAMPAIGN — ALL OF WHICH SET THE STAGE FOR AN ANTI-NETANYAHU CAMPAIGN, THE SENATE PERMANENT SUBCOMMITTEE ON INVESTIGATIONS SAID IN A BIPARTISAN STAFF REPORT.

This initiative taken by the Obama Administration is largely responsible for the frosty relationship that existed between the prime minister and President Obama. Despite the efforts of the Obama Administration to interfere in the 2015 Israeli election, Prime Minister Netanyahu and his right-wing Likud Party prevailed.

In early September 2017 Facebook announced that Russian-linked sources had spent $100,000 on political ads in 2015 and 2016. Details were made available to U.S. government authorities, presumably to Special Counsel Robert Mueller and congressional committees investigating Russian meddling in the 2016 presidential election.

According to a Facebook spokesperson, the ads were primarily issue-oriented and not for or against any specific candidate. It has been suggested that the real purpose of the advertising was to create political disruption and turmoil among the youth of America—the most dedicated and frequent users of Facebook—by presenting ads that take controversial positions on topics such as race relations, LGBT rights and gun control.

News of the Facebook ads stoked the heated voices of liberal commentators who were quick to bundle the revelation into the generalized narrative of Russian interference in the American political process, and that somehow the Trump Administration must have been behind it.

Mark Penn, author and political strategist, was one of the first to put the Russian-linked Facebook advertising in perspective. In an October 15, 2017, opinion piece in *The Wall Street Journal* entitled "You Can't Buy the Presidency for $100,000" the author wrote:

THE FAKE NEWS ABOUT FAKE NEWS IS PRACTICALLY ENDLESS. AMERICANS WORRIED ABOUT RUSSIA'S INFLUENCE IN THE 2016 ELECTION HAVE SEIZED ON A HANDFUL OF FACEBOOK ADS—AS THOUGH THERE WEREN'T ALSO THREE

90-MINUTE DEBATES, TWO TELEVISED PARTY CONVENTIONS, AND $2.4 BILLION SPENT ON LAST YEAR'S CAMPAIGN. THE DANGER IS THAT BENDING FACTS TO FIT THE RUSSIA STORY LINE MAY NUDGE WASHINGTON INTO NEEDLESSLY AND RECKLESSLY REGULATING THE INTERNET AND CURTAILING BASIC FREEDOMS.

Penn added that only 44% of the ads appeared prior to Election Day, and that most of the pre-election advertising was not targeted at swing states and did not mention a specific candidate. The impact of Russian-linked Facebook advertising was insignificant.

FUSION GPS IS AN INVESTIGATION and research firm based in Washington D.C., co-founded in 2011 by three former Wall Street Journal staff members. As a privately-held company, we don't know all of their past activities, but we do know the following:

- The Democratic Party hired Fusion GPS to conduct an opposition research investigation into Mitt Romney in advance of the 2012 presidential election. The investigation targeted a major contributor to the Romney campaign, Frank VanderSloot and his company Melaleuca. Criticism of VanderSloot's public statements about gay rights and of his company's multi-level marketing methods appeared in a February 2012 *Mother Jones* magazine article. A defamation suit filed against the magazine by VanderSloot was dismissed by the District Court in Idaho in 2015.

- In 2015 The Center for Medical Progress released undercover video reports purportedly showing Planned Parenthood officials discussing the practice of collecting and selling human fetal tissue obtained through abortions to medical researchers. The videos were acquired during meetings between Planned Parenthood and pro-life activists David Daleiden, founder of The Center for Medical Progress, and Sandra Merritt posing as potential buyers of fetal tissue.

  Planned Parenthood enlisted the services of Fusion GPS to help debunk the video reports which had become a source of embarrassment to the Planned Parenthood organization. Fusion GPS hired video and transcription experts to analyze the videos. Their report suggested that the videos had been heavily edited, purportedly to emphasize wrongdoing by Planned Parenthood officials.

While pro-life politicians requested a criminal investigation of Planned Parenthood, a Texas grand jury impaneled to look into the matter found no wrongdoing by Planned Parenthood, but instead brought an indictment against Daleiden and a coworker for attempting to purchase human organs. The charges in the Texas indictment were eventually dropped, but Attorney General for the State of California, Xavier Becerra, later charged Daleiden and Merritt with 15 felonies for failing to obtain consent of the individuals being recorded and criminal conspiracy to invade privacy. In June 2017, Judge Christopher Hite struck down the charges as being "too broad," but AG Becerra refiled the charges nine days later after individually correlating the "victims" of illegal reporting with specific videos. In a statement, AG Becerra said:

THE RIGHT TO PRIVACY IS A CORNERSTONE OF CALIFORNIA'S CONSTITUTION AND A RIGHT THAT IS FOUNDATIONAL IN A FREE DEMOCRATIC SOCIETY. WE WILL NOT TOLERATE THE

CRIMINAL RECORDING OF CONFIDENTIAL CONVERSATIONS.

Supporters of Daleiden and Merritt have claimed that Attorney General Becerra pursued the case against the pair because Planned Parenthood made contributions to several previous political campaigns of the AG. They have also complained that this is the first case in California where investigative reporters working to uncover possible wrongdoing have had to face charges of illegally recording the subjects of their investigation.

As of this writing, neither the criminal case nor a civil lawsuit brought against The Center for Medical Progress by Planned Parenthood has been adjudicated.

- Fusion GPS was hired in September 2015 by *The Washington Free Beacon* to conduct opposition research on Donald Trump and other Republican candidates, Matthew Continetti editor-in-chief of the *Free Beacon* confirmed on October 27, 2017. As a conservative political entity, it is possible but unconfirmed that the purpose was to vet the slate of the most promising

Republican candidates in order to uncover any facts that might later come out and prove embarrassing to the campaign. The task was terminated after Donald Trump emerged as the probable Republican candidate for president.

In an October 24, 2017, *Washington Post* article by Adam Entous, et al we learned that the international law firm, Perkins Coie LLP, retained by the Hillary Clinton campaign and the DNC, hired Fusion GPS to reopen and continue the opposition research study targeting Donald Trump. It has been suggested elsewhere that Fusion GPS approached the DNC with their earlier *Free Beacon* investigation of Republican candidates in order to reestablish an income stream from their prior work that had ended.

Fusion GPS hired Christopher Steele, former British intelligence MI-6 agent, to "uncover" any possible negative information about candidate Trump as well as identifying evidence of a Russian connection to the Trump campaign. A report based upon Steele's memoranda to Mark Elias of Perkins Coie submitted between June and December 2016 became known as the Trump-Russia Dossier.

The Trump–Russia Dossier contains unverified allegations of personal misconduct and collusion between the Russian government and the Trump election campaign. It has been reported that in late 2016, Senator John McCain delivered a copy of the dossier to then-FBI Director James Comey. It is not yet known if the dossier was a key factor in the decision to expand the investigation into Trump-Russia collusion and the decision to establish a special counsel to investigate.

On October 18, 2017, Fusion GPS officials Peter Fritsch and Thomas Catan appeared before the House Intelligence Committee where they invoked their Fifth Amendment right against self-incrimination and refused to answer questions about the Trump-Russia dossier.

The Clinton campaign and the DNC together have paid over $9 million to Perkins Coie for "legal and compliance consulting" from November 2015 until late October 2016. However, current DNC officials, including DNC Chairman Thomas Perez, have disavowed knowledge of any link between the Clinton campaign or the DNC and the

Trump-Russia Dossier. A DNC spokeswoman said:

TOM PEREZ AND THE NEW LEADERSHIP OF THE DNC WERE NOT INVOLVED IN ANY DECISION-MAKING REGARDING FUSION GPS, NOR WERE THEY AWARE THAT PERKINS COIE WAS WORKING WITH THE ORGANIZATION. BUT LET'S BE CLEAR, THERE IS A SERIOUS FEDERAL INVESTIGATION INTO THE TRUMP CAMPAIGN'S TIES TO RUSSIA, AND THE AMERICAN PUBLIC DESERVES TO KNOW WHAT HAPPENED.

Brian Fallon, a former spokesman for the Clinton campaign, said he was unaware that Fusion GPS was hired during the campaign. He stated:

THE FIRST I LEARNED OF CHRISTOPHER STEELE OR SAW ANY DOSSIER WAS AFTER THE ELECTION, BUT IF I HAD GOTTEN HANDED IT LAST FALL, I WOULD HAVE HAD NO PROBLEM PASSING IT ALONG AND URGING REPORTERS TO LOOK INTO IT. OPPOSITION RESEARCH HAPPENS ON EVERY CAMPAIGN, AND HERE YOU HAD PROBABLY THE MOST SHADOWY GUY EVER RUNNING FOR PRESIDENT, AND THE FBI CERTAINLY HAS SEEN FIT TO LOOK INTO IT. I PROBABLY WOULD HAVE VOLUNTEERED TO GO TO EUROPE MYSELF TO TRY AND VERIFY IF

IT WOULD HAVE HELPED GET MORE OF THIS OUT THERE BEFORE THE ELECTION.

When asked if Mrs Clinton knew of her campaign's association with Fusion GPS and the dossier, Fallon said she "may have known, but the degree of exactly what she knew is beyond my knowledge." A spokesman for Debbie Wasserman Schultz, Florida Congresswoman and former DNC chairperson, said that Wasserman Schultz had "no knowledge" of the arrangement with Fusion GPS.

18.

The Embodiment of Integrity

MY FRIEND CALLED ME ABOUT A personal matter on the very day in May 2017 that Robert Mueller was appointed by the justice department as the special counsel overseeing the investigation into Russian interference with the 2016 election and ties to Donald Trump's presidential campaign. Before we hung up she asked me what I thought of the appointment and of the man.

I told her that I am nearly always skeptical about why things like this—the very determination that a special counsel was needed—come about, and that I would have to reserve judgement. Regarding the particular choice of Robert Mueller, I knew very little about him, but the early reports were quite favorable. I had read that news of Mr Mueller's appointment was met with an enthusiastic response from members of both parties on Capitol Hill, where he was viewed as having been one of the most credible law enforcement officials in the country. A Washington D.C. defense attorney who had worked closely with Mr Mueller summed it up, saying that he was "the embodiment of integrity."

I was initially hopeful that the investigation would be completed expeditiously and in a completely unbiased and transparent fashion, but I had a few nagging concerns as enumerated below:

1. A TSUNAMI OF EFFUSIVE SUPPORT. This one was a bit difficult to wrap my head around. I sensed it that very first day while telling my friend about all the praise that was coming forth—not only for the decision to select a special counsel, but for Mr Mueller personally. It was as if the accolades had been carefully collected in bushel baskets, waiting to be showered down on a simple-minded public within nanoseconds after the announcement was made.

In the words of the old English bard, "Me thinks they praiseth too much."

2. THE FRIEND OF MY FRIEND IS MY FRIEND. Mr Mueller was nominated by President George W. Bush to be FBI Director in 2001 and was confirmed unanimously by the Senate. He began his term just one week before the 9/11 attacks and served for 12 years. James Comey succeeded him as FBI Director, and it has been reported that Mueller and Comey were best friends. Others have said their friendship was only work-related. Considering the tense relationship between President Trump and former FBI Director Comey, a close relationship between Mueller and Comey could be construed as a conflict of interest.

3. THE PREDATORS IN GREY WORSTED. It has been reported that at least seven of the 16 lawyers that Robert Mueller brought on to his special counsel team had donated to Democratic political candidates, five of them to Hillary Clinton, and zero donating to Donald Trump's campaign. Although this suggests a potential for anti-

Trump bias, Mr Mueller would have had a tough time finding a politically conservative attorney for his team as independent surveys indicate that more than 70% of our nation's attorneys favor liberal candidates and causes.

4. ALL POLITICS IS LOCAL. In early August 2017 it was reported that Special Counsel Robert Mueller had impaneled a Washington, D.C. grand jury for the probe into Russian interference in the 2016 election. Now, grand jurors understand that personal politics are to have no place in the grand jury room, but when one considers that Donald Trump won only 4% of the Washington D.C. vote in the 2016 election, it is likely that only one or two of the 23 grand jurors in that panel voted for Mr Trump. In retrospect, Mr Mueller might have considered impaneling a grand jury in suburban Virginia.

Oh, wait! Mueller's team had already been working with a grand jury in Alexandria, Virginia, left over from the Michael Flynn case. It was not clear whether both grand juries would continue their efforts in the

Russia probe, or if all work would eventually be transferred to the Washington D.C. panel.

5. With Donald Trump capturing only 4% of the vote in the District of Columbia and less than 18% in Alexandria City, maybe Mr Mueller should have considered impaneling a grand jury somewhere in Culpeper County instead. Yes/No?

6. SOMEBODY IS GOING TO JAIL. After assembling a team of 16 prominent attorneys and a support staff that must have numbered in multiple dozens, and after issuing numerous court orders and spending months gathering witness testimony, and after impaneling a second grand jury and presenting the evidence, and after spending millions of taxpayer dollars in this effort, does anyone believe for a minute that the final conclusion of this case would be, "Sorry, we've found nothing there."?

In an Op-Ed published at The Hill on August 7, 2017, attorney, author and former professor of law, Alan Dershowitz makes the case that the decision by Mr Mueller to impanel a grand jury in the

District of Columbia was a tactical one. Dershowitz writes:

> THE DECISION TO IMPANEL A SECOND GRAND JURY MAY HAVE LITTLE TO DO, THEREFORE, WITH THE WORK OF THE GRAND JURY, WHICH COULD HAVE JUST AS EASILY BEEN CONDUCTED A FEW MILES AWAY IN A NORTHERN VIRGINIA COURTROOM. IT MAY, HOWEVER, HAVE EVERYTHING TO DO WITH THE PETIT JURY THAT MAY EVENTUALLY BE SELECTED TO TRY ANY DEFENDANT WHO IS ULTIMATELY INDICTED.
>
> DEFENDANTS ARE BROUGHT TO TRIAL IN THE VENUE WHERE THEY ARE INDICTED. HAD THE VIRGINIA GRAND JURY REMAINED THE ONLY GRAND JURY INVESTIGATING THE RUSSIAN CONNECTION, THEN ANY CASES INDICTED BY THAT GRAND JURY WOULD HAVE BEEN TRIED IN VIRGINIA. BUT NOW THAT A SECOND GRAND JURY HAS BEEN IMPANELED IN D.C., ANY DEFENDANT INDICATED BY THAT GRAND JURY WOULD BE TRIED IN FRONT OF A D.C. PETIT JURY COMPRISED OF CITIZENS OF THE DISTRICT.

Mr Dershowitz went on to discuss the composition of the jury pool from which the petit jurors would be selected. On the subject of political party affiliation of the Washington, D.C. citizenry, Mr Dershowitz writes:

> THE DISTRICT OF COLUMBIA JURY POOL WILL BE OVERWHELMINGLY DEMO-CRATIC, BY A RATIO OF CLOSE TO 10 TO 1. THE VIRGINIA POOL IS LIKELY TO BE MORE DIVERSE IN ITS POLITICAL AFFILIATIONS, THOUGH PROBABLY STILL MORE DEMOCRATIC THAN REPUBLICAN.

He also intelligently addressed the sensitive issue of race and the significant role it can play in jury selection. For his trouble, Mr Dershowitz was unfairly criticized and called a racist by Congresswoman Maxine Waters, Democrat from California.

There had been early calls from the far-Right for special counsel Mueller to be fired or to recuse himself from the Russia investigation because (1) he delivered samples of enriched uranium to Russian operatives in 2009 and (2) he held investments in hedge funds and other financial instruments tied to Russian firms and Antifa financial backer, George Soros.

In fact, the uranium had been recovered as part of a joint sting operation with

Russian law enforcement, and a small sample of what was recovered—about one-third of an ounce—was sent to Moscow for analysis. Mueller was FBI Director at the time.

Regarding Mueller's investments, it would be unusual to be invested in any large mutual fund or exchange-traded fund that invests in international firms that doesn't have Russian and Eastern European companies as part of their portfolio. George Soros owns companies and is heavily invested in Eastern Europe.

As Hillary Clinton might say, "We've got a couple of nothing-burgers here."

WHEN THE MUELLER REPORT was finally issued in March 2019, we learned that while Russia had indeed attempted to influence the 2016 Presidential Election through computer hacking and the placement of advertising aimed at disrupting the American political process, there was no evidence of collusion between Trump election officials or the Trump administration with Russian government operatives. Disappointed over the conclusions of the Mueller Report, in December 2019 the Democratic-led U.S. House of Representatives approved articles of impeachment against the president, citing abuse of power and obstruction of Congress alleging that the president solicited foreign interference to aid his 2020 reelection bid. On February 5, 2020, the president was acquitted by the Senate.

19.
The Culture War

IT WAS UNCLEAR WHO HAD ISSUED THE ORDER TO STOP THE POLICE FROM INTERVENING IN PROTESTER ACTIVITIES, BUT WHEN THE CROWD REALIZED THAT THE POLICE WERE GOING TO STAND DOWN, THE VIOLENCE ESCALATED.

INDIVIDUALS WHO WERE DISCERNED AS REPRESENTING THE OLD ORDER WERE BEATEN WITH FISTS AND STICKS. PROTESTS IN SOME CITIES REACHED THE BRINK OF ANARCHY AND THE MILITARY HAD TO BE BROUGHT IN TO RESTORE ORDER.

THROUGHOUT LARGE REGIONS OF THE COUNTRY HISTORICAL SITES WERE VANDALIZED. PUBLIC MEMORIALS WERE REMOVED AND POSTERS TORN DOWN. THE NAMES OF CITY STREETS AND IMPORTANT BUILDINGS IN MANY COMMUNITIES WERE CHANGED TO THE NAMES OF THE NEW ORDER HEROES.

Does the previous narrative sound familiar? Is it describing activities in Charlottesville or Berkeley? What about the defacing and removal of Civil War Memorials in the South? Actually, it doesn't represent any of those places or things. Instead, it is a description of what actually took place in People's Republic of China during the Cultural Revolution that began in 1966.

The "protesters" in the narrative were the Red Guards, students who gathered in bands, marching through cities and the countryside in order to root out subversive political thought and activities. The Cultural Revolution was set into motion by Chairman Mao Zedong who saw factions in the government slowly abandoning the principles of Marx and Lenin in what was feared to be a movement toward capitalism.

Dissidents were sent to re-education camps and collective farms; the worst "offenders" were imprisoned and often killed. Historical relics and artifacts throughout the country were destroyed.

A September 7, 2011, *New York Times* article, "China's Reluctant Emperor", by author Sheila Melvin includes a photograph of the remains of a Ming Dynasty emperor where "Red Guards dragged the remains of the Wanli Emperor and Empresses to the front of the tomb, where they were posthumously denounced and burned."

While violence and upheaval spread across China in the1960s and 70s, a different sort of Cultural Revolution was taking place in the United States, ultimately responsible for bringing about much needed changes to laws and public opinion on issues such as voter rights, racial discrimination and women's equality.

Many of these causes were advanced by liberal thinking in the country, and the Democratic Party was quick to claim credit. Democrats succeeded in accomplishing two important objectives: (1) labeling Republicans as anti-woman, anti-gay, anti-black, anti-immigrant, and the party of the rich and privileged and (2) obscuring the historical fact that it was the Democratic Party that consistently resisted granting of equal rights to minorities. In a *Washington Times* Op-Ed by Jennifer Kerns published on August 18, 2017, the author gives examples:

- DEMOCRATS VOTED TO KEEP AFRICAN AMERICANS IN SLAVERY, OPPOSING THE 13TH AMENDMENT WHICH OFFICIALLY FREED THE SLAVES. ONLY FOUR DEMOCRATS VOTED FOR IT.

- REPUBLICANS ALSO PASSED THE 14TH AMENDMENT WHICH GRANTED SLAVES U.S. CITIZENSHIP; DEMOCRATS VOTED AGAINST IT.
- REPUBLICANS ALSO PASSED THE 15TH AMENDMENT WHICH GAVE SLAVES THE RIGHT TO VOTE. NOT A SINGLE ONE OF THE 56 DEMOCRATS IN CONGRESS VOTED FOR IT. . . .
- THE REPUBLICAN PARTY ITSELF WAS FOUNDED AS THE "ANTI-SLAVERY PARTY" IN 1854. THE PARTY SUBSEQUENTLY GAVE US PRESIDENT ABRAHAM LINCOLN AND ULTIMATELY, THE EMANCIPATION PROCLAMATION WHICH LED TO THE LIBERATION OF SLAVES.
- THE DEMOCRATIC PARTY WAS RESPONSIBLE FOR PASSING JIM CROW LAWS, IN ADDITION TO BLACK CIVIL CODES THAT FORCED AMERICANS TO UTILIZE SEPARATE DRINKING FOUNTAINS, SWIMMING POOLS, AND OTHER FACILITIES IN THE 20TH CENTURY.
- EVEN DEMOCRATIC ICONS SUCH AS KENNEDY VOTED AGAINST THE 1957 CIVIL RIGHTS ACT WHILE IN THE U.S. SENATE. SEN. AL GORE, SR., D-TENN., ALSO OPPOSED IT.

190

Nor should we forget that the president pro tempore of the Senate for three years ending in 2010—and for three prior periods throughout his career—was Richard C. Byrd, Democrat from West Virginia and former "Exalted Cyclops" of the Ku Klux Klan. Although it is worth noting that before his death, Byrd did express regret for his former association with the Klan.

QUESTION: WHEN DOES A CULTURAL Revolution become a Culture War? Answer: When the progressive forces of the revolution are met with great resistance; for example, when Donald J. Trump is elected president of the United States.

Some would argue, however, that the resistance started well before he was elected president and, indeed, was largely responsible for his victory. After the 2015 off-year elections for three Congressional seats and governorships and a variety of other state and local races and issues, an article, "Liberals are Losing the Culture War," by staff writer, Molly Ball, was published in *The Atlantic*. Ms Ball writes:

DEMOCRATS HAVE BECOME INCREASINGLY ASSERTIVE IN TAKING LIBERAL SOCIAL POSITIONS IN RECENT YEARS, BELIEVING THAT THEY ENJOY

MAJORITY SUPPORT AND EVEN SEEKING
TO TURN ABORTION AND GAY RIGHTS INTO
ELECTORAL WEDGES AGAINST
REPUBLICANS. BUT TUESDAY'S
RESULTS—AND THE BROADER TREND OF
RECENT ELECTIONS THAT HAVE BEEN
GENERALLY DISASTROUS FOR
DEMOCRATS NOT NAMED BARACK
OBAMA—CALL THAT VIEW INTO
QUESTION. INDEED, THEY SUGGEST THAT
THE LEFT HAS MISREAD THE
ELECTORATE'S ENTHUSIASM FOR SOCIAL
CHANGE, INVITING A BACKLASH FROM
MAINSTREAM VOTERS INVESTED IN THE
STATUS QUO.

Ms Ball provides several examples from that 2015 election that support her claim. Three of the items she cites are the following:

- OHIO VOTERS REJECTED A BALLOT INITIATIVE TO LEGALIZE RECREATIONAL MARIJUANA BY A 30-POINT MARGIN.
- VOTERS IN HOUSTON—A STRONGLY DEMOCRATIC CITY—REJECTED BY A 20-POINT MARGIN A NONDISCRIMINATION ORDINANCE THAT OPPONENTS SAID WOULD LEAD TO "MEN IN WOMEN'S BATHROOMS."

- THE SAN FRANCISCO SHERIFF WHO HAD
  DEFENDED THE CITY'S SANCTUARY POLICY
  AFTER A SENSATIONAL MURDER BY AN
  ILLEGAL IMMIGRANT WAS VOTED OUT.

In retrospect, Democratic Party operatives would have been well-advised to consider Ms Ball's examples as no less than a flock of asphyxiated canaries in a coal mine just before the roof fell in.

DOES IT CONTINUE? IS THE PRESIDENT fighting a Culture War against his opponents? In a September 25, 2017, *New York Times* article by Glenn Thrush and Maggie Haberman the authors write:

> IN PRIVATE, THE PRESIDENT AND HIS TOP
> AIDES FREELY ADMIT THAT HE IS
> ENGAGED IN A CULTURE WAR ON BEHALF
> OF HIS WHITE, WORKING-CLASS BASE, A
> NEW YORK BILLIONAIRE WAGING WAR
> AGAINST "POLITICALLY CORRECT"
> COASTAL ELITES ON BEHALF OF HIS
> SUPPORTERS IN THE SOUTH AND IN THE
> MIDWEST. HE BELIEVES THE WAR WAS
> FOISTED UPON HIM BY FORMER
> PRESIDENT BARACK OBAMA AND OTHER
> DEMOCRATS — AND HE IS DETERMINED
> TO WIN, CURRENT AND FORMER AIDES
> SAID.

The Culture War is not only continuing, but it has escalated. If you require more evidence, consider the 2017 words from an old(er) Culture Warrior, known for his provocative 1992 Republican National Convention culture war speech. Now, twenty-five years later, in an October 10, 2017, Real Clear Politics column, "Trump Embraces the Culture War," conservative political commentator, Patrick Buchanan writes:

> IN THE CULTURE WARS, TRUMP HAS REJECTED COMPROMISE OR CAPIT- ULATION AND DECIDED TO DEFEND THE GROUND ON WHICH HIS MOST LOYAL FOLKS STAND.
>
> EXAMPLE: WHILE THE *WASHINGTON POST* WAS REPORTING MONDAY THAT AUSTIN, SEATTLE, SAN FRANCISCO AND DENVER HAD NOW JOINED LOS ANGELES IN REPLACING COLUMBUS DAY WITH INDIGENOUS PEOPLE'S DAY, TRUMP ISSUED A COLUMBUS DAY PROC- LAMATION OF BRISTLING DEFIANCE.

If you are paying attention to what is going on around you, it is easy to see that the Cultural Revolution continues to impinge on life in America. Here are some examples:

- Applicants for admission to the University of California, are asked to answer to the following question, "How do you describe yourself? (Mark one answer)" Choices are:
  1. male
  2. female
  3. trans male/trans man
  4. trans female/trans woman
  5. gender queer/gender non-conforming
  6. different identity

- Many brick-and-mortar retail stores have replaced "Merry Christmas" in posters and customer greetings by sales personnel with "Happy Holidays."

- In some localities, a pedophile is no longer a pedophile; he (or she) is now a "minor-attracted person."

- Leaders at Christ Church in Alexandria, Virginia, where George Washington attended services decided that a memorial plaque marking the pew where Washington sat with his family must be removed because it makes some visitors feel unsafe or unwelcome because Washington was a slaveholder.

- In California, those who work in health care who use the wrong gender pronoun when referring to a transgender patient could be fired or even face prison time.

- A Seattle school renamed its Easter eggs, 'spring spheres', to avoid causing offense to people who did not celebrate Easter.

- A Boy Scouts of America official says they will admit girls to the Cub Scouts and establish a program for older girls.

- The Southern Poverty Law Center lists the Family Research Council and several evangelical Christian ministries as hate groups but fails to track organizations such as Occupy Wall Street because, according a SPLC spokesperson, "We're not really set up to cover the extreme Left."

- The Dallas Independent School District is exploring the renaming of schools named after Benjamin Franklin, Thomas Jefferson and James Madison because of their historical ties to slavery.

- A University of Minnesota professor and a St. Paul, Minnesota, therapist jointly published a manifesto declaring Donald Trump a unique threat to America's mental health. More than 3,800 therapists signed the on-line document.

The previous list is evidence that the Cultural Revolution in America is not abating.

In 2017 I wrote that, "We should expect—if the first several months of the Trump Administration are any indication—that the Cultural Revolution in America will likely transform itself into a full-blown Culture War as opposing political forces clash, resisting the programs, ideas and legislation proposed by the other." We need only look at recent efforts to erase our history by toppling statues, changing the names of sports teams and military bases, and seemingly endless civil unrest in U.S. major cities to affirm that prediction.

20.
What Now?

THERE IS NO DENYING THAT FORCES exist both within and outside America that desire nothing less than to have President Trump removed from office. At first, it was thought that if only some major wrongdoing committed by the president could be uncovered, he would be obliged to step down in shame. If he refused, then articles of impeachment could be brought against him. Surely, it was thought, that the special counsel assigned to investigate Russian interference in the election could find some evidence of criminal activity or serious wrongdoing.

As months passed absent any new revelations of wrongdoing, and with no hint that the president himself had become a target of the special counsel investigation, the president's enemies became frustrated. The Sunday edition of the *Washington Post* on October 15, 2017, contained a full-page ad placed by *Hustler* publisher Larry Flynt. The headline of the ad read in large, boldface type:

$10 MILLION FOR INFORMATION LEADING TO THE IMPEACHMENT AND REMOVAL FROM OFFICE OF DONALD J. TRUMP

On October 20, 2017, California billionaire environmentalist Tom Steyer announced plans to spend at least $10 million for a nation-wide television advertising campaign calling for the impeachment of President Trump. Steyer, a banking and hedge fund mogul, was a major donor to the Democratic Party. He had a petition calling for the impeachment of President Trump at the website action.needtoimpeach.com. A statement on the site read:

DONALD TRUMP HAS BROUGHT US TO THE BRINK OF NUCLEAR WAR, OBSTRUCTED JUSTICE, AND TAKEN MONEY FROM FOREIGN GOVERNMENTS. WE NEED TO IMPEACH THIS DANGEROUS PRESIDENT. **ADD YOUR NAME.**

At the time, the site claimed more than 500,000 signatures. There was also an impeachdonaldtrumpnow.org website sponsored by two organizations, Free Speech for People and RootsAction. The site claimed more than 1.2 million signatures. In 2017 a Google search of the phrase "impeach Donald Trump" returned nearly 400,000 results.

WITH THIS MUCH ACTIVITY SEEKING TO impeach or otherwise remove the president from office, it should be no surprise that there were also individuals suggesting that it was still possible for Hillary Clinton to become the occupant of the Oval Office well before the end of the current presidential term.

In an October 13, 2017, posting at Medium.com by Harvard Law Professor Lawrence Lessig, the author describes a scenario whereby Hillary Clinton could replace Donald Trump as the current president of the United States. In the piece entitled "IF {THAT} THEN {THIS}" Professor Lessig poses and then presents an answer to the question, "what should happen if Trump conspired with a foreign government to get elected? If he did that, then what should happen?"

In an October 16, 2017, Newsweek article by Julia Glum, "HOW HILLARY CLINTON STILL CAN, AND SHOULD, BECOME PRESIDENT AFTER THE TRUMP-RUSSIA INVESTIGATION," the author summarizes Professor Lessig's hypothetical path forward for Hillary in a scenario of five if/then eventualities. I have inserted the "THEN" that was "missing" from the first four "IF" statements by Ms Glum:

IF NUMBER 1: IF TRUMP IS DEFINITIVELY FOUND TO HAVE COLLUDED DIRECTLY WITH RUSSIA, [THEN] HE WOULD BE FORCED TO RESIGN OR BE IMPEACHED.

IF NUMBER 2: IF TRUMP IS REMOVED, [THEN] VICE PRESIDENT MIKE PENCE WOULD BECOME PRESIDENT.

IF NUMBER 3: IF PENCE BECOMES PRESIDENT, [THEN] HE SHOULD RESIGN TOO, GIVEN THAT HE BENEFITED FROM THE SAME HELP FROM MOTHER RUSSIA.

IF NUMBER 4: IF PENCE RESIGNS BEFORE APPOINTING A VICE PRESIDENT, [THEN] RYAN WOULD BECOME PRESIDENT.

IF NUMBER 5: IF RYAN BECOMES PRESIDENT, HE SHOULD DO THE RIGHT THING AND CHOOSE CLINTON FOR VICE PRESIDENT. THEN HE SHOULD RESIGN.

While the gist of the *Newsweek* piece was supportive of Professor Lessig's points, several other writers expressed agreement only with a single statement from the professor's original article; that is, "I realize this all sounds crazy right now. . . ." Rush Limbaugh was critical of the Lessig article during his radio talk show, resulting in angry responses to the medium.com posting from Rush listeners, some of whom questioned the professor's fitness to teach law.

In a lengthy rejoinder from the professor added later as a preface to the original posting and repeated in a Fox News interview with Tucker Carlson, Professor Lessig claimed that the original article was written and posted only "after receiving questions about what should happen if the Mueller investigation yields specifically damaging evidence about the president." Now, while that may be an accurate statement, you should know that Professor Lessig was not shy concerning his thoughts about President Trump and what he'd like to see become of the Trump presidency. Professor Lessig was a member of the Legal Advisory Board of the Impeach Trump Now initiative at impeachdonaldtrumpnow.org mentioned earlier in this chapter.

In an interview with National Public Radio as part of her *What Happened* book tour, Mrs Clinton was asked if she had ruled out the possibility of challenging the results of the presidential election. Her answer was that she wouldn't completely rule it out, but added:

> THERE ARE SCHOLARS, ACADEMICS, WHO HAVE ARGUMENTS THAT IT WOULD BE [POSSIBLE TO CHALLENGE THE RESULTS], BUT I DON'T THINK THEY'RE ON STRONG GROUND. BUT PEOPLE ARE MAKING THOSE ARGUMENTS. I JUST DON'T THINK WE HAVE A MECHANISM.

Summarizing my own past thoughts concerning the possible path to a Hillary Clinton presidency à la Lawrence Lessig, for whatever reason the article was posted, one would need to be dwelling in a state of conscious suspension of reality to believe that the IF/THEN scenario described by Professor Lessig might actually come to pass. Or, as Scooby-Doo is apt to say, *"Huh?"*

IN A SEPTEMBER 2017 INTERVIEW WITH "Sunday Morning" anchor Jane Pauley on CBS, Mrs Clinton said, "I am done with being a candidate. But I am not done with politics because I literally believe that our country's future is at stake."

Hillary Clinton's remarks lead one to wonder, "What does the future hold for the Democratic Party?" It took only a few short months after the election for Donald Trump to disassemble much of what President Obama and the Democrats were able to achieve in the eight years after Obama's promise to "fundamentally transform the United States of America." The failure to repeal and replace Obama's Affordable Care Act is a notable exception.

As the Democratic Party seems to be sliding further left, it is curious to consider in August 2020 just how Joe Biden became their standard bearer. In a December 27, 2016, article by Niall Stanage, the author listed the top 15 Democratic presidential candidates for 2020, as ranked by The Hill:

1. Senator Elizabeth Warren (Massachusetts)
2. Senator Bernie Sanders (Vermont)
3. Senator Cory Booker (New Jersey)
4. Senator Amy Klobuchar (Minnesota)

5. Senator Kirsten Gillibrand (New York)
6. Former first lady Michelle Obama
7. Governor John Hickenlooper (Colorado)
8. Senator Chris Murphy (Connecticut)
9. Former Vice President Joe Biden
10. Governor Andrew Cuomo (New York)
11. Senator Kamala Harris (California)
12. Former Sec of State Hillary Clinton
13. Former Governor Deval Patrick (Massachusetts)
14. Senator Tim Kaine (Virginia)
15. Oprah Winfrey

The author of the article did not provide the ranking criteria that were used by The Hill, but it appears that the candidates that ranked higher on the list were the most left-leaning, and ranking points were deducted for losing a recent national election.

One of the more interesting ticket combinations that gained some attention in 2017 was Biden-Sanders. A July 2017 Public Policy Polling survey predicted that either Joe Biden or Bernie Sanders could defeat Donald Trump in 2020, and a ticket featuring both men could do very well. The survey results indicated that about one out of every eight voters who would pick Biden or Sanders over Donald Trump had actually voted for Trump in 2016.

Survey results may be interesting, but in the opinion of many, even with the economic disruption caused by the COVID-19 pandemic, Donald Trump may be hard to beat in 2020. It is worth noting that on Election Day 2020, Donald Trump will be 74 years old and Joe Biden 77.

IN THE CONTINUING MATTER OF FUSION GPS, it is still not known if the three degrees of separation between Hillary Clinton/DNC and Christopher Steele, the individual who was hired to prepare the Trump-Russia Dossier, will be sufficient to provide Hillary and DNC officials with a shield of "plausible deniability" in this matter. Up until the present, they have either chosen not to comment (Hillary) or have denied knowing about it (DNC). The degrees of separation are illustrated below:

Hillary/DNC to

Mark Elias/Perkins Coie to

Fusion GPS to

Christopher Steele to

???

Whether or not the connection between Fusion GPS and the DNC/Hillary Clinton campaign (or Uranium One and the Clinton

Foundation) is ever subject to a criminal investigation and prosecution, we can expect the media to ignore or minimize any potential scandal of the Left. Meanwhile, Donald Trump Jr meeting with a Russian lawyer during the election campaign is tantamount to treason.

The irony in the disparity of media treatment with respect to the two campaigns is expressed succinctly in an October 17, 2017, *Investor's Business Daily* editorial:

> IT'S STRANGE THAT AN INVESTIGATION CONTINUES INTO THE INCONSEQUENTIAL TIES BETWEEN THE DONALD TRUMP CAMPAIGN AND RUSSIAN OFFICIALS, WHILE SOLID EVIDENCE OF BRIBERY OF THE CLINTON FAMILY BY THE RUSSIANS AND MANY OTHERS IS COMPLETELY IGNORED.

In May 2019, Attorney General William Barr announced that the U.S. Attorney from Connecticut, John Durham, had been tasked to look into the origins of the FBI's Trump-Russia investigation known as "Crossfire Hurricane." Justice Department Inspector General Michael Horowitz had been conducting his own investigation for more than a year into possible wrongdoing in the FBI's investigation of the Trump presidential campaign.

At this point in the Durham investigation, we know that it has been expanded to include elements of the U.S. intelligence community. It is not known if any results of Durham's investigation will become public prior to the November 2020 election.

More Titles from Sky Scientific Press

CONVERGENCE

A time travel novel by Thomas Settimi
Paperback ISBN-13: 978-1-4196-6151-8
eBook Edition 2012

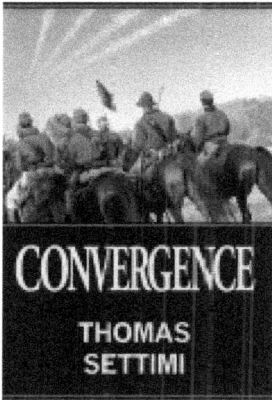

The feathery white ribbons in the sky high above Adams County in Pennsylvania were nothing unusual—just the vapor trail evidence of high-flying aircraft that one might see on any day. But for the men on the ground below they were a puzzlement. And no wonder: the year was 1863 and the men were Confederate soldiers marching toward the most significant battle of the American Civil War.

Thousands of miles away and 105 years later, Navy pilot Nathaniel Booth and his navigator complete their air mission over Laos and are headed back to the deck of the *USS Enterprise* when their aircraft mysteriously vanishes. Our hero Booth is declared Missing in Action. Years later when Rose Booth, the family matriarch, learns that her son may not have been a casualty of the war as previously believed, she enlists a prominent history professor and his protégé to uncover the truth.

In this carefully researched historical novel with a cosmic twist, the author traces the convoluted struggle to weave together the threads of a lost airman's life and bring solace to a grief-stricken mother.

ROSWELL 1947

A time-travel novel by Thomas Settimi
Paperback (ISBN-13: 978-0-6158-2917-3)
eBook Edition 2013

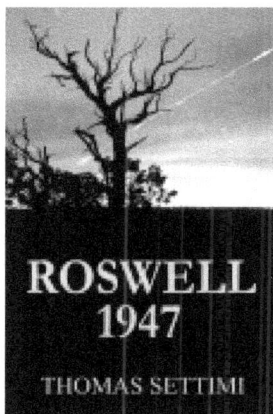

After helping solve the very strange case of a Vietnam-era pilot caught up in a cosmic disruption in time and space as described in the author's novel, *Convergence*, Professor Roger Atwood and Amanda Marshall are off on a new quest.

In 1947, Colonel Dieter Hedrick was a young lieutenant serving in the Public Information Office at Roswell Army Air Field, New Mexico. As one of the last surviving witnesses to the strange events that occurred in July of that year, he calls upon investigative reporter, Amanda Marshall, to tell his story of the Roswell Incident.

Upon hearing the Colonel's compelling, yet incomplete, account of the events that occurred more than sixty years ago, Amanda enlists the assistance of Professor Roger Atwood to settle the issue once and for all.

Were we really visited by aliens? Was there a government cover-up? In this fast-paced novel based on the often-told story and speculation surrounding the Roswell Incident, the author presents a startling alternative explanation for one of the most controversial events of the last century.

Roswell 1947 is a sequel to the author's novel, *Convergence.*

BEAK OF THE TURTLE

A novel by Thomas Settimi
Paperback ISBN-13: 978-0-6922-1080-2
eBook Edition 2014

They came from the stars—from a place in the night sky known to the ancients as the "Beak of the Turtle." They came to Earth in search of their roots and found a civilization that had just begun to stir.

In 1953 Professor Tsum Um Nui was employed as an instructor and researcher in the Anthropology Department at Beijing University. At the urging of a colleague, the professor embarked on a challenging task: translating microscopic symbols engraved on a few ancient stone burial discs. The discs—eventually known as "Dropa Stones"—were discovered by his colleague during a 1938 expedition to the Bayan Har Mountains near the China-Tibet border.

Despite the astonishing nature of his findings, Professor Tsum earned little acclaim for his work; first due to the stifling repression of the Cultural Revolution and later when his findings were deemed to be inconsistent with the philosophy and image of the Chinese Communist Government.

More than fifty years later, the Professor's daughter seeks the assistance of investigators Roger Atwood and Amanda Marshall *(characters from Convergence and Roswell 1947)* to document the life's work of her father and restore his blemished reputation.

Beak of the Turtle is a story of ancient aliens and the quest of modern day investigators to find and interpret the evidence they left behind 4,600 years ago.

THE AVIARY

A novel by Thomas Settimi
Paperback ISBN-13: 978-0-6925-1687-4
eBook Edition 2015

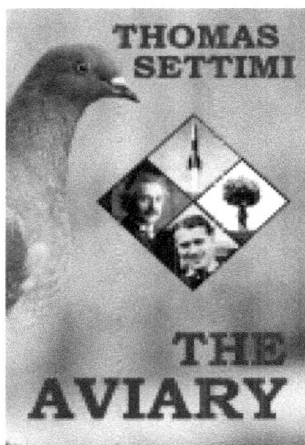

Pamela Devereux and her Grandson Jason watched the feathered visitors swoop down to the old weathered aviary on the deck of her Southern California mountain home. The aviary door had disappeared long ago, and the birds could come and go freely, attracted by the bowls of fresh water and birdseed that Pamela refilled daily.

When a young Rock Pigeon returns to the aviary again after several recent visits, Pamela recalls the strange events that began twenty years earlier: How a visitor to the aviary from another time helped to save her son, the father of Grandson Jason.

The Aviary is a tale of alternate history and the unintended consequences that follow as countries in conflict race to develop terrible new weapons of war.

BEYOND 2020: A story of liberty lost, hope and recovery

A novel by Thomas Settimi
Paperback (**ISBN-13:** 978-1074544676)
eBook Edition 2019

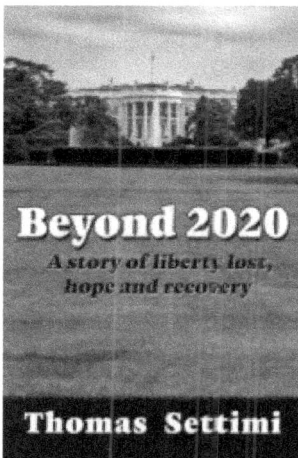

No one could have predicted it.

After nearly four years marked by an impressive list of accomplishments — even in the face of harsh resistance from the opposition party — the Trump administration looked forward to successfully completing the final year of the president's first term, winning re-election and moving on to four more years of service to the country and her people.

What, then, could possibly have derailed the President's plan, denying him what was believed to be an assured victory in November 2020?

"Elections have consequences," we are reminded. In the months and years that followed, the voices of Talk Radio sounded the warning that the New Socialism would methodically suppress the freedoms promised in the Constitution, but it would take an America at the brink of revolution to restore what was lost.

USER GUIDE TO AUTHOR & PUBLISHER MANUSCRIPT MAKER V 4.0: Transform a Draft of Your Novel or Non-Fiction Book into a Ready-to-Publish Kindle EBook, ePub File or Print PDF

By Thomas Schriftsteller
eBook Edition 2017

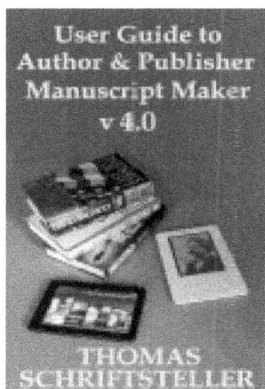

This How-To publishing and formatting guide was written for use with the "Author & Publisher Manuscript Maker" software application for Personal Computers published by Sky Scientific Press. It permits authors/self-publishers to create and manage electronic and print book projects.

If you are a new author just learning about Print-On-Demand and ePublishing or a published author with multiple titles interested in improving the professional appearance of your work, this useful guide may be for you.